On Memory, Marriage, Tears, and Meditation

READING AUGUSTINE

Series Editor:
Miles Hollingworth

Reading Augustine offers personal and close readings of St. Augustine of Hippo from leading philosophers and religion scholars. Its aim is to make clear Augustine's importance to contemporary thought and to present Augustine not only or primarily as a pre-eminent Christian thinker but as a philosophical, spiritual, literary, and intellectual icon of the West.

Volumes in the series:
On Music, Sense, Affect, and Voice,
Carol Harrison
On Solitude, Conscience, Love and Our Inner, and Outer Lives,
Ron Haflidson
On Creation, Science, Disenchantment, and the Contours of Being and Knowing, Matthew W. Knotts
On Agamben, Arendt, Christianity, and the Dark Arts of Civilization, Peter Iver Kaufman
On Self-Harm, Narcissism, Atonement, and the Vulnerable Christ,
David Vincent Meconi
On Faith, Works, Eternity, and the Creatures We Are,
André Barbera
On Time, Change, History, and Conversion, Sean Hannan
On Compassion, Healing, Suffering, and the Purpose of the Emotional Life, Susan Wessel

On Memory, Marriage, Tears, and Meditation

Margaret R. Miles

BLOOMSBURY ACADEMIC
LONDON • NEW YORK • OXFORD • NEW DELHI • SYDNEY

BLOOMSBURY ACADEMIC
Bloomsbury Publishing Inc
50 Bedford Square, London, WC1B 3DP, UK
1385 Broadway, New York, NY 10018, USA

BLOOMSBURY, BLOOMSBURY ACADEMIC and the Diana logo are trademarks of
Bloomsbury Publishing Plc

First published in the United States of America 2021

Copyright © Margaret R. Miles, 2021

Margaret R. Miles has asserted her right under the Copyright, Designs and Patents Act, 1988, to be identified as Author of this work.

For legal purposes, the Acknowledgments on p. xi–xii constitute an extension of this copyright page.

Cover design: Terry Woodley
Cover image © Wladimir Bulgar, Science Photo Library/Alamy Stock Photo

All rights reserved. No part of this publication may be reproduced or transmitted in any form or by any means, electronic or mechanical, including photocopying, recording, or any information storage or retrieval system, without prior permission in writing from the publishers.

Bloomsbury Publishing Inc does not have any control over, or responsibility for, any third-party websites referred to or in this book. All internet addresses given in this book were correct at the time of going to press. The author and publisher regret any inconvenience caused if addresses have changed or sites have ceased to exist, but can accept no responsibility for any such changes.

A catalogue record for this book is available from the British Library.

Library of Congress Cataloging-in-Publication Data
Names: Miles, Margaret R. (Margaret Ruth), 1937- author.
Title: On memory, marriage, tears, and meditation / Margaret R. Miles.
Description: New York, NY, USA : Bloomsbury Academic, 2021. | Series: Reading Augustine | Includes bibliographical references and index. | Summary: "On Memory, Marriage, Tears, and Meditation offers readers the tools for reading Augustine's journey to human emotions through his writings on feeling, marriage, conversion, and meditation. Augustine understood that feeling, not rationality, gathers and reveals the deep longing of the whole person. Throughout his ecclesiastical career, he discussed marriage in sermons, letters, and treatises from the perspective of his own experience. Miles examines Augustine's prototypes for conversion - reading and conversion; sacrifice and conversion; and the importance of friends in what might be considered a subjective and private process. Meditation was central to Augustine's Christian life and Miles argues that his practice of meditation suggests that penitence included a rich range of feeling leading to gratitude, peace, wonder, and love"–
Provided by publisher.
Identifiers: LCCN 2020045378 (print) | LCCN 2020045379 (ebook) |
ISBN 9781350191426 (pb) | ISBN 9781350191433 (hb) |
ISBN 9781350191440 (epub) | ISBN 9781350191457 (epdf)
Subjects: LCSH: Augustine, of Hippo, Saint, 354-430. | Emotions–Religious aspects–Christianity. | Christian saints–Algeria–Hippo (Extinct city)–Biography.
Classification: LCC BR65.A9 M55 2021 (print) | LCC BR65.A9 (ebook) | DDC 270.2092–dc23
LC record available at https://lccn.loc.gov/2020045378
LC ebook record available at https://lccn.loc.gov/2020045379

ISBN:	HB:	978-1-3501-9143-3
	PB:	978-1-3501-9142-6
	ePDF:	978-1-3501-9145-7
	ePUB:	978-1-3501-9144-0

Typeset by Integra Software Services Pvt. Ltd.

To find out more about our authors and books visit www.bloomsbury.com and sign up for our newsletters.

CONTENTS

Preface vi
Acknowledgments xi
Texts and Translations xiii
List of Abbreviations xiv

1 Augustine: Theologian of Feeling 1
2 Augustine's *Coniugium* 19
3 Augustine's Conversions 33
4 Bodies, Pleasures, and the Young Augustine 55
5 Augustine's Meditation 73
6 Augustine's Deathbed Tears 89

Notes 102
References 107
Index 111

PREFACE

Reading for Life

We read for many reasons, for information, for entertainment, for curiosity; we read for ideas, and we read critically to analyze and evaluate the author's argument. We read to understand others' thoughts and values, and to see how others live. We read to see what it feels like to be in another body, another place, another time. We read both desperately and playfully, trying on in imagination other ways of feeling and doing than those to which we are accustomed.

We read for life, to gather the knowledge we need in order to answer for ourselves the ancient question, how should we live? In *David Copperfield*, Charles Dickens's protagonist recalls:

> The picture rises always in my mind, of a summer evening, the boys at play in the churchyard, and I sitting on my bed, reading as if for life.
>
> (*Dickens*, 52–3)

Augustine's *Confessions* relates several reading experiences—Augustine's own and others'—that instantaneously and permanently altered the reader's life (*conf.* 8. 5–12). These events were often provoked by a scripture verse: the prototypical desert ascetic, St. Antony, *heard* the verse, "Sell all that you have, give to the poor, and follow me," and he obeyed. Augustine, in the middle of his anguished conversion to celibacy, *heard* a short scriptural passage, "Put on the Lord Jesus Christ, and make no provision for the flesh" (Rom. 13:14), that resolved his indecision. He tells of others whose copycat conversions were prompted simply by hearing stories of others' reading-for-life conversions. In each case, the conversion moment was preceded by long periods of anxiety, unhappiness, and searching.

In short, we read to gather experiences and perspectives that our particular lives, our gendered bodies, social location and parenting, our education and experiences have not provided. We read most intentionally and intensely when we bring the pressured interests of our own lives to our reading. Only then does the text speak directly to its reader in its most vivid and powerful language; only then does its abstract language "collapse into immediacy" (Collingwood: *The Idea of History*); only then is it heard *in corde meo*. The text must resound

> there, *there* in the place where I had been angry with myself, inside, in my own room, there where I had been pierced, *there* where I had made my sacrifice, offering up my old self, and starting on the purpose of a new life, with my hope set on you [God] —*there* it was where you began to grow sweet to me ... I cried out as I read this with my outward eye and inwardly recognized its truth. (*conf.* 9. 4)

When heard *in the heart*, the "dead" or abstract text speaks directly to the questioner in the immediacy of her or his life. The reader's questions bring to this conversation the desperate energy, not of intellectual puzzles, but of feeling: it is the reader's *feeling* that precipitates the collapse into immediacy. "All we need is some light to read by" (Richards, *Centering*, 146).

Augustine's mentions of angels are few and far between; angels appear in scripture, so he must accept their existence, but they do not have a speaking part in the story of his life. As if to recommend the practice of reading, however, Augustine said that angels read, although they "have no need of reading to understand": "They read; they choose; they love; their reading is perpetual, and what they read never passes away ... their book is never closed" (*conf.* 13. 15).

Readers for life practice a double process of interpretation. We bring our experience to understanding a text, and we invite the text to question our experience. Augustine's *Confessions* exemplifies this dual interpretation. On the one hand, he wrote: "My personal experience enabled me to understand what I had read" (*conf.* 8. 5; 7. 16). On the other, he allowed the text to judge his experience: "The more ardent was the love I felt for those men [who had renounced public life and marriage], the more bitter was the hatred I felt for myself when I compared myself with them" (*conf.* 8. 6). Augustine learned, by his "own experience," that reading can change a life.

Reading "as if for life" is critical reading, questioning not only the text, but also other interpretations that inevitably notice some features while ignoring—or simply not seeing—others. This is especially true of a text like Augustine's *Confessions* that has been read and interpreted for more than fifteen hundred years. *Every* interpreter approaches the *Confessions* with a complex perspective composed of vastly different experiences, education, institutional affiliations, race, gender, social location, age, and other variables too many and too subtle to name. Furthermore, a text as evocative as Augustine's *Confessions* inevitably attracts readers' passionate responses, a range of which are invariably articulated in any situation in which it is discussed.

Augustine Reading Augustine

Several years before his death, Augustine undertook to review his published works. In his *Retractationes* (*Reconsiderations*) Augustine critically examined many of his publications, correcting infelicitous or, he feared, misleading language. He reread his writings in roughly chronological order, intending to include in his survey, not only treatises, but also his sermons and letters. However, distracted by other duties, he did not complete his project. Having reviewed ninety-three of his publications, he abandoned the project in 427 CE, three years before his death. Thirty years after he wrote his *Confessions*, the autobiography of his youthful struggle, he said the following in his *Reconsiderations*:

> The thirteen books of my confessions praise the just and good God for *both the bad and the good that I did,* and they draw a person's mind and emotions toward him. As for myself, that is how they affected me when they were being written, and that is how they affect me when they are being read. What others may think of them is up to them, but I know that they have pleased and do please many of the brothers a good deal. (*retr.* 2. 6)

Why was *Confessions* pleasurable reading for Augustine? Surely the first nine books recount thoughts and actions of which the old bishop might reasonably be dismayed. And surely the brothers who were pleased by Augustine's confessions did not find his youthful transgressions edifying. The answer, I think, is that Augustine enclosed "both the bad and the good that I did" (*malis et bonus meis*) *within* God's unerring leading (*conf.* 11. 2). *This* was the narrative that gathered and wove together the colorful strands of his life. God's omnipresent leading was the "cover story" within which Augustine collected his memories, a narrative capacious enough to exclude *none* of his experience.

Chapter 5 explores the origin of Augustine's story in his practice of meditation, articulated in *Confessions*, but fully understood only at the end of his life. Augustine's meditations involved his memories of the people and events that informed his feeling, recalled and *repurposed* to explain and support his story, namely, that from infancy God's omniscient and utterly trustworthy leading shaped the apparently random circumstances of his life.

Interpreting Augustine

Any interpreter should begin by acknowledging the perspective from which she or he reads Augustine. This requirement is especially true for an interpreter who reads for life, attuned to some features of a text with exquisite attentiveness, while overlooking others. I have read Augustine hungrily, "for life," for more than fifty years. When I was twenty-two, a painful ulcer that threatened to perforate led me to psychotherapy, and psychotherapy led me to education. At this time, I read Augustine's *Confessions*, and the energy that had been chewing my stomach lining was diverted to my head, to thinking. The ulcer disappeared and has not recurred. I have learned enormously, reading voraciously and promiscuously, from Augustine, his interpreters, many other authors, and, most importantly, from life.

More than a decade ago I wrote *Augustine and the Fundamentalist's Daughter*, a reflection on my engagement with Augustine in my youth. Now I am older than Augustine ever was, and I read a different Augustine, one who *became* Christian across a lifetime, who lived long enough to reflect on that experience, to describe it, and to be profoundly grateful. My experiences, the people I love, and my feeling inform my reading of Augustine. In the following chapters, I will describe several of my experiences that are especially pertinent to my reading of Augustine. I hope that others may be provoked to read Augustine "for life."

The first chapter of the first book of Augustine's *Confessions* evokes a feeling, all-too-familiar to many people—insomnia, restlessness, twisting and turning, inability to lie quietly and await sleep. A terrible restlessness and its resolution bookend *Confessions*: "You [God] have made us for yourself, and our hearts are restless (*inquietum*) until they rest in you" (*conf.* 1. 1). Augustine described the content of his narrative: "My foolhardy soul went away from you: It has turned indeed, over and over, on back and side and front, and always the bed was hard, and you alone are rest" (*conf.* 6. 16). The last book of *Confessions* reports the resolution of Augustine's restlessness:

> Our rest is our place … Things are moved by their own weights and go to their proper places. When at all out of their place, they become restless; put them back in order and they will be at rest (*quiescent*). My weight is my love; by it I am carried wherever I am carried, it is my love that carries me there.
>
> (*conf.* 13. 9)

I have mentioned the significance of *feeling*. Chapter 1 discusses Augustine's understanding of feeling (*adfectus*) and its role in shaping the self, bringing to prominence a feature of Augustine's thought that has often been understood as a side effect of his intellectual journey. I suggest that feeling should be considered essential and fundamental to his self-understanding.

ACKNOWLEDGMENTS

Augustine lived in a time when wars, disease, lack of internal police, and childbearing were common dangers, but the natural world—the created world—seemed to him invulnerable. He remarked in a sermon, "The world is a smiling place" (s. 158. 7). As I write, the pandemic Covid-19, ecological danger, climate change, homelessness, and endangered species threaten the earth and its inhabitants. In our time, harms inflicted by human greed and carelessness must also be feared.

If the coronavirus brings any wisdom, it can only be to make the vulnerability of living creatures evident and urgent. Bodies R us; as Plato observed, we are not called mortals for nothing. Susceptibility to disease and death is a condition of human life that the privileged can usually conceal from consciousness in order to "get on with it." Pandemic disease prompts our abstract knowledge of death to "collapse into immediacy." No one is immune. We become, as never before, consummately grateful for the precious yet fragile gift of life, urging us to treat ourselves, our loved ones, and our unknown neighbors with kindness. We are reminded daily to love the world that God *so loved*.

This book began as the Annual St. Augustine Lecture at Villanova University in October 2019, "St. Augustine's Deathbed Tears: Recollecting and Reconsidering a Life." Friends at the Augustinian Institute were generously appreciative of the lecture and suggested that I expand it into a book. Wanting to continue to explore the apparently limitless wealth and beauty of Augustine's life and thought, I agreed to do so. I am profoundly grateful for the fellow pilgrims whose conversations have stimulated, questioned, and delighted me, especially Professor Martin Laird O.S.A. and Professor James Wetzel, Director of the Augustinian Institute at Villanova University. Dr. Ian Clausen, editor of *Augustinian Studies*, graciously gave permission to include articles published in the journal. Dr. Miles Hollingworth, editor of the "Reading Augustine" series for Bloomsbury Academic, has been an encouraging companion and champion for the book. I am grateful to Gordon Gilmore for research assistance, and to Laura Dunn for formatting the manuscript.

My lifelong indebtedness to Augustine can be summarized in his words: "Delight is, as it were, the weight of the soul. For delight orders the soul; where the soul's delight is, there is its treasure" (*Delectatio quippe quasi pondus est animae. Delectatio ergo ordinat animum ... ubi delectation, ibi treasaurus; mus.* 6. 11. 29).

June 1, 2020
Berkeley, California

TEXTS AND TRANSLATIONS

Unless otherwise noted, English translations of Augustine's *Confessions* are from Rex Warner (1963), *The Confessions of St. Augustine*, Mentor Books. Translations of passages from *The City of God against the Pagans* are from R. W. Dyson, ed. and trans. (1998), Cambridge University Press. *On Christian Doctrine* translations are from D. W. Robertson (1958), Bobbs-Merrill. Translations from Augustine's *Expositions of the Psalms* are by Maria Boulding, O.S.B. (2000), New City Press. John Burnaby, ed. and trans. (1955), *Augustine: Later Works*, Library of Christian Classics, Westminster Press, for English translations of Homilies on the First Epistle of St. John. Short translations from several treatises are from Erich Przywara, arranged and trans. (1958), *An Augustine Synthesis*. P. G. Walsh, ed. and trans. (2001), Latin and English quotations from *De bono coniugali; De sancta uirginitate*. English quotations from *De Praedestinatione sanctorum* and *De dono perseuarantiae* are by Peter Holmes (1956), for Saint Augustine's Anti-Pelagian Works, NCPNF. Stephen McKenna's *C.S.S.R.* (1970) was used for English translations of *On the Trinity*.

I used Latin editions available to me, usually *Patrologia Latin*, Migne (1845), and CSEL. For Augustine's *The Confessions of Augustine*, John Gibb, ed. (1908), Cambridge Patristic Texts: Cambridge University Press. Translations from Possidius are from *Sancti Augustini Uita*, ed. and trans. Herbert T. Weiskotten (1919).

ABBREVIATIONS

conf.	*Confessiones*
c. Iul.	*Contra Iulianum*
an. et or.	*De anima et eius origine*
beata u.	*De beata uita*
b. coniug.	*De bono coniugali*
ciu.	*De ciuitate dei*
cont.	*De continentia*
corrept.	*De corruption et gratia*
doct. chr.	*De doctrina christiana*
perseu.	*De dono perseuerantiae*
f. et symb.	*De fide et symbol*
Gn. litt.	*De genesi ad litteram*
mor.	*De moribus ecclesiae*
mus.	*De musica*
praed. sanct.	*De praedestinationes sanctorum*
an. quant.	*De quantitate animae*
uirg.	*De sancta uirginitate*
spir. et litt.	*De spiritu et littera*
trin.	*De Trinitate*
util ieiun.	*De utilitate ieiunii*
ench.	*Enchiridion*
ep.	*Epistulae*
ps.	*Ennarrationes in Psalmos*
praed. sanct.	*Praedestinatione sanctorum*
retr.	*Retractationes*
s.	*Sermones*
Io. eu. tr.	*Tractatus in Ioh. Eu.*
ep. Io. tr.	*Tractatus in Epistolam Ioannis*

1

Augustine: Theologian of Feeling

St. Augustine's *Confessions* often narrates the young Augustine's intellectual quandaries over philosophical questions, such as the origin of evil and the operations of memory and time, but the text is *continuously* propelled by Augustine recollecting and reliving his *feeling* at particular moments, and his analysis of how his feeling was triggered and altered. The earliest and most fundamental of his gifts, he said, were life and feeling: "Even then I had a being; I lived and I felt" (*conf*. 1. 20). He recalled many childhood feelings vividly and in detail, and he did not wear rose-colored glasses when remembering and observing infancy and childhood. He found the infant's hard work of birthing, and the child's acclimatization to the world of human society, strenuous indeed: "Who would not tremble and wish rather to die than to be an infant again if the choice were put before him?" (*ciu*. 21. 4)

When he was nineteen years old, he read Cicero's *Hortensius:* "It was this book which *altered my feeling (mutauit adfectum meus)*, turning my prayers to you, Lord, yourself, and gave me different ambitions and desires." A powerful feeling consumed him: "I was inflamed (*flagrantia*) ... I was on fire (*ardebam*) to leave earthly things behind and fly back to you [God]." Even in the heat of passion, however, Augustine missed any reference to Christ, whose name he had "drunk in devoutly" (*biberat pie*) with his mother's milk, and "it remained deeply treasured" (*conf*. 3. 4). It was not intellectual curiosity that urged him forward on his journey to becoming Christian. It was strong feeling.

Augustine on Feeling

The role of feeling is key to understanding Augustine's *Confessions*. "What exactly was this feeling?" (*conf.* 2. 9) He distinguished between momentary emotions, provoked by events, and *feeling*, the expression of him*self*. He was often annoyed and dismayed by uncontrollable rogue emotions. For example, his mother's death created a split in Augustine's feeling. His reason told him that she was (as they say), "in a better place," but he could not contain his tears: "I was deeply vexed that these human feelings should have power over me ... and I grieved at my grief with a new grief and so was consumed with a double sorrow." Emotions overwhelmed him; he drowned in his grief rather than rejoicing that "she did not die in misery, nor was she altogether dead" (*conf.* 9. 12). His youthful irritation at his mother's insistent interference in his life dissolved in his sorrow at her loss. He loved her. His grief inspired one of the most intimate and tender eulogies written by a son for his mother in Western literature (*conf.* 9. 13).

However, feeling (singular), as St. Augustine used the word, is not the same as emotions, nor is it the same as feelings (plural). Everyday usage does not help to express this very significant distinction. Augustine used the singular noun "feeling" (*adfectus*) to describe a cluster of intellect, emotions, and body. Feeling collects and expresses desire, belief, perceptions of beauty, regret, gratitude, delight, and more. Rationality is part of feeling, but is neither dominant nor decisive. In Augustine's usage, feeling *gathers, reveals, and directs the deep longing of the whole person*.

The idea of feeling as a heterogeneous mass of emotions and intellect was a profoundly counter-cultural idea for philosophers of antiquity, challenging their instinct to identify and differentiate phenomena. Plato said that lacking organization and clear distinctions "what you are bound to get ... is not real mixture but literally a miserable mass of unmixed messiness" (Philebus 1147e). Romans called the contents of the sewer under Rome *"mixtus"* (Miles, 2009: 80).

It is commonplace today to think of rationality as separate—and to be carefully sequestered—from feeling. We must jettison this assumption if we are to begin to understand Augustine, his contemporaries, and his followers. For Augustine, feeling was a settled disposition, a coordinated and weighted energy that focuses and directs the intention of the self. To refer to this integrated expression of self, I will use "feeling." To distinguish, as Augustine did, between feeling and emotions, I will use "emotions" to designate externally provoked "feelings."

At its most strongly concentrated—that is, not distracted by multiple and conflicting desires—Augustine recognized feeling's intention as a longing for *more life*. He said in a sermon:

> I know you want to go on living. You do not want to die. And you want to pass from this life to another in such a way that you will not rise again as a dead person, but fully alive and transformed. This is what you desire. *This is the deepest human feeling.* Mysteriously, the soul itself wishes and instinctively desires it.
>
> (*s.* 314. 4; emphasis added)

Augustine came to understand *by his experience* that feeling, not intellectual persuasion, was both the site of his own subjectivity and the location of God's direction of his life (*conf.* 7. 16). He attempted to describe a fundamentally ineffable feeling that is him*self,* relating two occasions on which he experienced what modern readers might call "mystical experiences." (*conf.* 7. 17; 9. 10)

> And sometimes working within me you open for me a door into a state of feeling which is quite unlike anything to which I am accustomed—a kind of sweet delight which, if I could only remain permanently in that state, would be something not of this world, not of this life. But my sad weight makes me fall back again; I am swallowed up by normality.
>
> (*conf.* 10. 40)

Those are not the only moments of powerful feeling in the *Confessions*, however. When Augustine recalled moments of strong feeling, he not only remembered but also relived those moments. Multiple times, in the middle of describing an incident or a thought—in *Confessions* or in a sermon or letter—he was suddenly overcome with feeling, interrupting his narrative, he burst out: "Turn us, O God of hosts, show us thy countenance and we shall be whole" (*conf.* 4. 10); "O eternal truth and true love and beloved eternity! You are my God" (*conf.* 7. 10); "O beauty of all things beautiful!" (*conf.* 3. 6). His text is peppered with such ejaculations of feeling.

Augustine loved the Psalms, commenting on them shortly after his conversion and for the next three decades (until 421 or 422 CE). Like Augustine, medieval monks loved the Psalms because of their expression of strong feeling.

> How loudly I cried out to you, my God, as I read the psalms of David, those faithful songs and sounding syllables of holiness quite excluding the swelling boastfulness of the spirit! ... How I cried aloud to you in those psalms! How they fired me toward you! How I burned to utter them aloud, if I could, to the whole world against the pride of mankind!
>
> (*conf.* 9. 4)

Misused Emotions

Because Augustine believed that God ordered his life through his feeling, he had strong objections to exploitation of the emotions. As a youth, he had been carried away (*rapiebant*) by stage plays: "I, poor wretch, at that time loved to feel sad and went looking for something to feel sad about." Reflecting on his experience later, however, he thought it crazy (*insania*) that people derive pleasure from viewing "miserable and tragic happenings which they would certainly not like to suffer themselves" (*conf.* 3. 2). He found this pleasure perverse. It is noteworthy that he did not object to stage plays because of their content, although Roman theater notoriously featured wicked acts and lewd scenes. He was dismayed, rather, by the manipulation of fake sympathy.

Augustine knew why he was entertained by fictional characters' sorrows; he understood why he enjoyed most of all "an actor who brought tears to my eyes." The displacement of genuine sorrow onto a fictional character briefly alleviated his own deep and unfocused sadness. Although he found momentary relief in weeping over fictional sorrows, Augustine nevertheless resented this manipulation. He also distinguished his feeling from the loud and volatile emotions displayed by crowds for "a famous charioteer or a fighter with wild beasts in the theater." My love (*amabam*) was not like that, he wrote: "it was different and more serious" (*sed longe et grauiter*). Indeed, his violent metaphors suggest the pernicious depth of his attraction. Fictional sorrow "scratched the surface of my skin ... [with] poisoned nails ... [producing] feverish swellings, abscesses, and running sores" (*conf.* 4. 14).

Compassion (*miserichordia*), an emotion Augustine valued very highly, should not, he said, be squandered on imaginary miseries. True compassion, he wrote, does not enjoy others' sufferings, but wishes that "they did not exist" (*conf*. 3. 2). "Is compassion, then, to be cast out?" he asks and answers, "Certainly not!" Augustine recognized that false compassion, created by enjoyment of fictional miseries, comes from the same root as the foundation of friendship. But emotions are not innocent; compassion, a good, can also lead to "foul lust." Emotions must be interrogated: "See where it leads; in what direction does it flow?" (*conf.* 4. 14; *ps.* 121. 1).

Bodies and Feeling

In his youthful rhetorical training, St. Augustine had startled his teachers with his ability to interpret Aristotle's *Ten Categories*. Aristotle may have alerted Augustine to the connection of bodies and emotions: "The soul's passions all seem to be linked with a body, as the body undergoes modifications in their presence" (Aristotle, *De anima* IA. 1. 403a. 15). Whether guided by Aristotle or by his own observation, Augustine noticed this connection. Throughout *Confessions*, he narrates life-changing moments as showcased in his body. His famous conversion to celibacy was one such occasion, characterized by an emotional storm acted out in his body. The restlessness that began his *Confessions* (1. 1) was at its most intense in this conversion. Augustine stated repeatedly that the restlessness that precipitated his conversion to celibacy was not an intellectual crisis. His mind, he said, was perfectly made up: "there was no longer any reason for me to doubt" (*conf.* 7. 10); "now I could see it perfectly clearly" (*conf.* 8. 5); "now the truth is certain" (*conf.* 8. 7). Rather, his conversion to celibacy vividly demonstrates the critical significance of feeling.

In Chapter 3, I discuss Augustine's conversion to celibacy as one of many conversions—conversions extending long before, and long after, his conversion to celibacy. Each conversion involved crucial shifts in his feeling. Together they were moments in his long process of *becoming Christian*. Augustine knew that celibacy was not required: "Not that the apostle forbade me to marry, though he might recommend something better" (*conf.* 8. 1). Nevertheless, his conversion to celibacy was a climactic event, for sex was the cherished pleasure without which Augustine could not imagine him*self*.

His so-called crisis of the will (*uoluntas*) was a crisis of feeling, "so went the controversy in my heart—about self, and self against self" (*ista controversia in corde meo non nisi deme ipso aduersus me ipsum*; *conf.* 8. 11). In his childhood and youth, both his parents had urged him to pursue "marriage and worldly success." Marriage to a wealthy and well-connected wife would have advanced Augustine's worldly success considerably. But according to his own testimony, it was sex, not marriage, that Augustine desired (*conf.* 6. 15). By the time Augustine reached young adulthood, Monica's hope for him had changed; she hoped that his sexuality would be stabilized in marriage so that he could be baptized (*conf.* 6. 13).

By the time of his conversion to celibacy, his desire for marriage and worldly ambition, conjoined in his mind as "slavery to the affairs of this world" (*conf.* 8. 6), was already modified by his interest in celibate monastic communities: "I no longer had the impulse and encouragement of my old hopes and desires for position and wealth ... these things no longer pleased me" (*conf.* 8. 1). All Augustine's questions and objections had melted away; the battle for "himself" was focused on his feeling, divided between two pleasurable attractions he considered incompatible—sex, which in retrospect he called the "violence of habit" (*conf.* 8. 11), and "If I want, I can be a friend of God now, this moment!" (*conf.* 8. 6). In what follows I turn to two themes which recur as leitmotivs throughout Augustine's description of his lifelong process of becoming Christian: humility and beauty.

Humility

Clearly, humility was central to Augustine.

> The way is firstly humility, secondly humility, and thirdly humility. And however you should ask me I would say the same, not because there are no other precepts to be explained, but

if humility does not precede and accompany and follow every good work we do, and it is not set before us to look upon, and beside us to lean upon, and behind us to fence us in, pride will wrest from our hand any good work we do while we are in the very act of taking pleasure in it.

(*ep.* 118. 3)

Why was humility of central importance to St. Augustine? His intelligence, education, social location, achievement as a teacher of rhetoric, and prizewinner in rhetoric contests in Milan did not foster humility. Nor did his education or the classical authors he read. Augustine reported that as a youth, he was "puffed up with knowledge" (*insuper autem inflabar scientia*; *conf.* 7. 10). He was a proud man: "I was separated from you by the swelling of my pride. It was as though my cheeks had swollen up so that I could not see out of my eyes" (*conf.* 7. 7).

"I had not the faintest notion of the mystery contained in 'The Word was made flesh'" (*conf.* 7. 18, 19). In Etienne Gilson's apt phrase, Augustine "discovered" humility (1960: 227) in the figure of Jesus Christ, who revealed humility—"divinity in the weakness that it had put on by wearing our 'coat of skin' ... [thus] healing the swelling of pride, and fostering love." Christ's humility was decisively established by his willingness to accept human flesh, "making a humble dwelling out of our clay." But as yet, Augustine confessed, "I was not humble enough to possess Jesus in his humility and weakness" (*conf.* 7. 17). For Augustine, the primary and lasting importance of Jesus was not his miraculous birth, not his teaching, nor his raising the dead to life; his example of humility was. "All Christians should hold fast to humility because they derive their name Christians from Christ; and no person who studies his gospel carefully fails to find him the teacher of humility" (*uirg.* 33). Christ's humility was fully demonstrated in his assumption of a human body, thus granting humans participation in his divinity.

Augustine believed that he had seen the truth, but he recognized the vast difference between seeing the way and being able to follow it. "I tried to find a way of gaining the strength necessary for enjoying you, and I could not find it until I embraced that Mediator ... the man, Christ Jesus." He realized that humility is necessary if he was to follow the humble Jesus.

I found that one is not only instructed so as to see you ... but also so as to grow strong enough to lay hold on you, and he who cannot see you for the distance, may yet walk along the road by which he will arrive and see you and lay hold on you.

(conf. 7. 21)

Humility was to become a recurring theme of Augustine's teaching and preaching. He described humility as a learning posture, if you think you *know* you are not likely to learn. Pride, the vice that opposes humility, creates blindness, "eyes swollen shut." Augustine associated pride with what Plato called "the double ignorance." Plato wrote: "This ignorance, which thinks that it knows what it does not, must surely be ignorance most culpable" (*Apology* 79 b-c). Augustine's version of the double ignorance is the following:

You can see how much it would have profited you if you had only known how to be ignorant in what you didn't know, and how this profit is still open to you ... Understand what it is you don't understand, lest you understand nothing, and don't despise anyone who, in order that he may understand, understands that he doesn't understand what he doesn't understand.

(an. et or. IV. 11. 15)

Humility became central to Augustine's feeling; his ongoing openness to lifelong learning depended on it. "I would rather say: 'I don't know' when I don't know" (*conf.* 11. 12). The scripture verse he quoted more frequently than any other throughout his ministry, I Corinthians 13:12, is further evidence of his commitment to humility, acknowledging the limitation of present vision: "We see now (*nunc*) through a mirror darkly; then (*tunc*) however, face to face." The present condition of human vision is, at best, distorted—*perspectival.* Only resurrected eyes will see clearly, *facie ad faciem.* Augustine commented on this verse when he imagined the resurrection in *City of God* XXII. 29.

I was a hospice volunteer for seven years. Sylvia, a 93-year-old Russian Jew, was one of my patients. In her youth, her father had owned a small business in Chicago, and Sylvia worked with him. One day her father was in a back room when a burglar entered the store. Hearing his voice, Sylvia's father came to the front. She shouted at him to stay back, but he continued to approach, was shot, and died instantly. In the days that followed, her mother and older brother "fell apart." "I wanted to collapse too," Sylvia said, "but I had too much to do. I had to be strong." She, a teenager, had to manage the funeral arrangements, the business, and the family. Many years later, as I left her home every day, she admonished me, "Be strong." Strength is a *choice*, she said. I had thought that you either *were* or *weren't*. But she insisted, "Strength is a choice."

Augustine, however, had a penchant for weakness, for weakness, like humility, kills pride. He often used metaphors of infant weakness to illustrate the receptive stance of a Christian before God. "What am I even at my best except an infant suckling the milk you give and feeding upon you, the food that is imperishable?"*(conf.* 4. 1). "I am only a little child, but my Father lives forever" (*conf.* 10. 4). Narrating his conversion to celibacy, he imagined Lady Continence saying: "Why do you try to stand by yourself, and so not stand at all? Do not be afraid. He will not draw away and let you fall. Put yourself fearlessly in his hands" (*conf.* 8. 12). In his mature writings, the weakness of old age replaced the infant's weakness: "Why be afraid that he may desert you, that he may toss you aside in your old age, when your strength has failed? That is precisely the time when his strength will be in you, when your own is gone" (*ps.* 70. I. 11).[1] Augustine's weakness was a necessary feature in his life story of God's productive activity in his life.

Augustine and Sylvia were both right; Augustine's metaphors suggest more than his prose describes. Sylvia and the infant trust *in and for the moment*; they do not boast a prideful *possession* of strength, but a breathless "I think I can." What I learn from my sense that both are right is that there are two kinds of strength: *will power*, the teeth-gritting strength founded on pride; "*I can and I will.*" And there is the tensile strength of weakness that acknowledges a need for help, whether the divine help for which Augustine prayed, or Sylvia's confidence that since she had a job to do, the needed strength would be accessible. This is strength that is not *possessed*, but received *as needed*.

Beauty

Augustine both learned from and challenged the classical authors he had studied. He incorporated, critiqued, and finally rejected every philosophy that did not include the name of Christ. Nevertheless, ancient philosophies crept back into his thinking. Augustine was "the conduit ... for a whole range of classical learning that would have been burnt and trodden to dust by the barbarians had it not turned up all over his writings" (Hollingworth, 2013: 33).

Beauty is one subject on which Augustine differed from philosophers. According to classicist Aryeh Kosman, Plato and Aristotle thought of beauty as primarily a moral category, used to describe "the natural beauty of persons and the beauty ... of their actions, and states of character" (Kosman, 247). Aristotle wrote: "Life should not be beautiful and therefore good, but good and therefore beautiful" (quoted by Kosman, 248). Objects were also considered beautiful, but their beauty proved difficult to define. Plato's only treatise on beauty, *Greater Hippias*, explores proposals from Socrates's interlocutors about what quality makes an object beautiful. Lengthy discussion did not result in a satisfying answer, so Socrates offered the inconclusive conclusion, "The beautiful things are difficult" (*Greater Hippias* 304e).[2]

Perhaps beauty cannot be objectively identified by its qualities but, Plato said, we know it when we see it! We know it *by the feeling it produces in us*:

> When one ... beholds a godlike face or bodily form that truly expresses beauty, first there comes upon him a shuddering and a measure of that awe which the vision inspired, and then reverence as at the sight of a god .... Next, with the passing of the shudder, a strange sweating and fever seizes him. For by reason of a stream of beauty entering in through his eyes there comes a warmth, whereby the soul's plumage is fostered.
>
> (*Phaedrus* 250e–251a)

The Platonic philosopher, Plotinus, agreed that beauty cannot be identified as a quality of an object, but only as a feeling experienced in its presence:

> But there must be those who see this beauty by that with which the soul sees things of this sort, and when they see it they must be delighted and overwhelmed and excited ... These experiences must occur whenever there is contact with any sort of beautiful thing, wonder, and a shock of delight, and longing and passion, and happy excitement.
>
> (*Ennead* 1.6.1)

Augustine thought about beauty within a different conceptual framework. In the literature of antiquity, "sunsets, meadows, groves and streams, waterfalls and fields of daffodils" were not described as beautiful. Augustine, however, thought of nature as *created*. He described himself as desperately questioning the earth, the sea, creeping things, blowing breezes, air, heaven, sun, moon, and stars: "Tell me about my God." They replied: "'He made us.' *My question was in my contemplation of them, and their answer was in their beauty*." Augustine's informants insisted: "We are not the God for whom you are looking" (*conf*. 10. 6; emphasis added). He understood by their answer that God, the "beauty of all things beautiful" (*conf*. 3. 6), is exhibited in God's creation.

Augustine's urgent question created the "collapse into immediacy" by which he saw the beauty of the created world *in the life*, as the tangible reflection and revelation of the creator's beauty. Immediacy was made possible, first, by the right question—Augustine's tenacious question; second, the questioner must understand the answer. "We are responsible for what we learn how to see" (Haraway, 1997: 289). The questioner must *see* the beauty of its creator in creation; that is, she must see the world *as creation* (Miles, 1983: 125–42). Look at creation, Augustine said, and you will *see* concrete evidence of God; God is not a metaphor, an allegory, or an abstraction. Beauty is the *link* that *connects* God and creation (*conf*. 10. 6).

My father loved his garden. His garden was his solace in the middle of life as an immigrant to the United States—a country whose values he did not share—from a farm in eastern Canada. His little plants (often housed in old shoes), sunflowers larger than a man's head, and tall corn stocks pleased him enormously. Every time I visited him as an adult, I reserved several hours to follow him around his half-acre garden while he explained each plant, why he had placed it where it was, its growth potential, and how it interacted with surrounding plants. Midway through our tour, he would stop, suddenly overwhelmed with the garden's beauty, and say with utmost scorn, "And they say there is no God!" Then we walked on.

In the same chapter in which he described his dialogue with creation, Augustine described the natural world, seen as creation:

> What do I love when I love you (God)? Not the beauty of the body nor the glory of time, not the brightness of light shining so

friendly to the eye, not the sweet and various melodies of singing, not the fragrance of flowers and unguents and spices, not manna and honey, not limbs welcome to the embraces of the flesh; it is not these that I love when I love my God. And yet I do love a kind of light, melody, fragrance, food, embrace when I love my God; for he is the light, the melody, the fragrance, the food, the embrace of my inner self—there, where is a brilliance that space cannot contain, a sound that time cannot carry away, a perfume that no breeze disperses, a taste undiminished by eating, a clinging together that no satiety will sunder. This is what I love when I love my God.

(*conf*. 10. 6)

This passage does not—as has sometimes been said—suggest the inferiority of the bodily senses by contrast with interior delights. Rather, Augustine can best express his delight and gratitude for the interior senses by evoking the rich pleasures of the bodily senses. The pleasure experienced from physical objects does not act merely as an apt analogy to inner delights; pleasure acts rather as a *connection* to the creator of the delightful physical world enjoyed by the senses. Interior pleasure is an extension and intensification of physical pleasure.[3] The senses both reveal and *participate* in inner pleasure: "The inner man knew these things by means of the ministry of the outer man. I, the inner man ... knew them through the senses of my body. I asked the whole mass and frame of the universe about my God and it replied, 'I am not he, but he made me'" (*conf*. 10. 6). In short, "What one loves and desires depends upon how one sees" (Astell, 2006: 106).

Beauty and Tears

Male socialization in Augustine's society permitted men to weep (Nagy, 2017: 16). Tears were understood to be a mark, not of weakness, but of strong feeling. In *Confessions*, Augustine reported incidents of episodic or circumstantial tears. Most of the tears of his youth were of this kind: tears of frustration (*conf*. 1. 6), of physical pain (9. 4), of grief over the death of a beloved friend (4. 4–7; 9. 12–13), of jealousy (3. 1), of grief over his mother's death

(9. 11–12), and sentimental tears over a fictional character (3. 2). Possidius, his contemporary biographer, reported that Augustine also wept at his conscripted ordination; others found these tears difficult to interpret (*Uita* 4, n. 9). However, the tears described in c*onf.* 8. 12 were not prompted by external circumstance, but by an acute emotional and intellectual crisis of compunction and conversion.[4]

Augustine also wept in the presence of beauty. He unselfconsciously reported his tears at the time of his baptism (*conf.* 9. 6). He also shed tears prompted by the sweetness of psalms sung in church (*conf.* 10. 33). Augustine, a man of strong feeling, did not hesitate to express him*self* in tears. Chapter 5 explores the importance of tears in Augustine's practice of meditation. In Chapter 6, I discuss his deathbed tears, bringing his practice of meditation to a reconsideration of the complex content of those tears. Augustine's tears, tears of repentance, his biographer said, included a much broader repertoire of feeling than the word connotes in modern usage. Augustine's deathbed tears were informed by his meditation, the practice in which he communed with his God.

Reading Augustine

Readers of Augustine's *Confessions* inevitably bring experience—whether acknowledged or not—that reveals features of the text that may be invisible to other readers. It is equally probable that modern readers misinterpret ancient authors due to our own cultural blinders. Can our conceptual differences *help* rather than distort our understanding of Augustine's *feeling* of his life?

Augustine said, "Anyone who cares to can read what I have written and interpret it as he likes" (*conf.* 9. 12). My experience helps me to read a different text than has been read by readers who thought it necessary to sequester their own experience from their interpretation of a man who lived more than fifteen hundred years ago in vastly different social and religious circumstances. However, this interpretive asceticism requires that the reader must not read "for life," must not bring her own questions and feeling to her reading. My metaphor for a mutually fruitful "conversation" between reader and text is from Homer's *Odyssey:* Odysseus visits the underworld, seeking answers to his desperate questions; the dead circle about him, but they cannot speak until he brings them bowls of blood (life) to drink. Temporarily nourished, they respond eagerly to Odysseus's questions. Just so, I believe that an abstract or dead text will speak ardently to a reader only when she brings her life to it.

My training as an intellectual historian did not encourage me to read "for life." Augustine taught me this. Not only did he repeatedly acknowledge that he understood "through my own experience" (*conf.* 4. 2; 8. 5), but he also encouraged others to do so. His *Homilies on the First Epistle of John* repeatedly urged his congregation to "ask your own heart" in order to access the immediacy of his teaching (*ep. Io. tr.*, 7th homily; also *ps.* 98. 3). He both cited his experience as a "hermeneutical principle" and recognized that his rendition of his life was vulnerable to interpretation by others with different experience. Interpretation of an author always, and simultaneously, exposes the interpreter's values, evident in what she or he has "learned how to see."

Many centuries after Augustine, another important Western philosopher described his *Meditations* as an exploration, not of *what can be known*, but of what *I* can know. Like Augustine, René Descartes considered personal interest an important component of rational inquiry. Long before the significance of perspective was acknowledged in universities, Descartes wrote, "Differences in opinion are not due to differences in intelligence, but merely to the fact that we use different approaches and consider different things" (*Discourse* 1. 2). Fruitful study is necessarily first-personal.

> It seemed to me that I would find much more truth in the reasoning that each person makes about the matters which are of concern to him, and of which the outcome is likely to punish him soon after he has made a mistake, than of those which a man of letters makes in his study, concerning speculations that lead to no result, and will have no other consequences for him, except perhaps that he will be all the more vain about them the further they are from common sense.
> (*Discourse* 1. 6. 9–10)

The following observations illustrate my suggestion that a reader's experience makes aspects of a text that other readers may not notice, pop into the eye.

I have mentioned that I hear, in Augustine's saga of becoming Christian, not one dramatic conversion (usually called simply "Augustine's conversion"), but many incremental conversions before and after his conversion to celibacy. Why did I notice Augustine's many conversions? "I understood by my own experience" of more than a decade of effective psychotherapy many years ago, that lasting change doesn't usually happen in a flash (*conf.* 7. 16). Change is more likely to occur, rather, in the incremental, often painful, sometimes boring, work of remembering and *reliving* painful experience. In so doing, one *converts* experience into thought, rather than acting it out in repetitive and unproductive patterns.

I read the *Confessions* as Augustine doing precisely that: retracing, articulating, and reliving a painful journey. The series of conversions I now notice were, of course, always in his text, but I did not notice them as long as I accepted other readers' consensus that "Augustine's conversion" (*conf.* 8. 12) was his only such experience. In Chapter 3, I explore Augustine's cumulative conversions, occurring not in one histrionic moment, but in many less dramatic but equally significant episodes of realization and integration.

It has also been said that the only actor in the *Confessions* is God. Again, alerted by my experience of psychotherapy to the long and difficult work of fundamental and lasting change, I notice Augustine's commitment and *hard work* as well as what he reports as God's irresistible leading. In his last writings, Augustine was still trying to articulate a delicate balance between God's action and his own struggle, not one agent doing something *to* another, but the interaction, the conversation, for Augustine the lifelong drama of the *relationship* (*praed. sanct.* 6).[5]

When does an interpreter's experience distort or interfere with the text rather than enable and energize understanding? The twentieth-century French philosopher Michel Foucault said: "My point is not that everything is bad, but that *everything is dangerous*, which is not exactly the same as bad. If everything is dangerous, then we always have something to do" (quoted in Dreyfus and Rabinow, 1983: 231–2). Everything is dangerous. Certainly, it is irresponsibly "dangerous" to assume that a text must reflect or challenge one's own experience. The text is not about *me*. My life is not the point. The text does not address me, cares nothing about me, and does not seek to help me. Yet the text *does* help me by requiring that I temporarily forget my busy search for information about myself. I must "relax a little from myself" (*conf.* 7. 14), from expecting to see my own favorite character in fiction, myself, in the text. If I am to understand what the author struggles to communicate, I must lay my agenda aside. Only after doing this may I notice where the text touches me, where it calls forth my feeling, where it says something to me that I can *use*.

Psychoanalysts speak of a fundamentally revised understanding of oneself as inevitably marked by a "narcissistic wound" to the belligerently self-confident ego. But "understanding" is not the right word; it seems to imply an "insight" registered by intellect. The "wound" is not to the intellect, but rather to one's self-*feeling*. A frightening sense of bottomless worthlessness accompanies fundamental new life-learning. It is experienced as a painful lack "there," in the *self*, "in my own room" (*conf.* 9. 4). No one describes the moment more vividly than Augustine:

> You ... were turning me around so that I could see myself; you took me from behind my own back ... you set me in front of my own face so that I could see how foul a sight I was—crooked, filthy, spotted, and ulcerous. I saw and I was horrified, and I had nowhere to go to escape from myself ... I did know it, but I pretended that I did not. I had been pushing the whole idea away from me and forgetting it.
>
> (*conf.* 6. 7)

Virginia Woolf's novel *Orlando* explores the observation that a single human life of seventy, eighty, or even ninety years is simply not long enough to learn everything one needs to know to be a human being. A lifetime is too short to gather the requisite experience. Experience is perspectival, heavily determined by multiple factors, such as male or female embodiment and socialization. It is difficult or impossible to imagine what life feels like in that other body. But bodies are only the beginning of our limitations, inattentiveness, shortsightedness, and incapacity for feeling. We struggle to supply these privations. We read; we ponder the arts; we love our families and friends as best we can; in short, we try.

I began to study Augustine because I wanted to understand why, although he had been a much-revered author in most of Western history, so many of my contemporaries disliked him. Pondering this, I concluded that when we find an author who so fulsomely describes his feeling, we are initially attracted, as to a kindred soul.

When we notice, however, that he too had the limitations of his body, his society, his emotional and intellectual education, we are disappointed. We complain that he did not share the sensibilities of *our* society, that he was overly respectful of authority, that he did not listen to women, and that he defended doctrines we don't like. We are miffed; he has seduced and disappointed us. This scenario, I think, goes at least part of the way toward explaining the animosity against Augustine to be found in various niches of twenty-first-century Western society and culture.

It is to be expected that an ancient text will be "heard" differently by readers in different circumstances. It is possible, however, to gather suggestions for life from a text that could not have anticipated my situation and how it might usefully be addressed. If, on the other hand, I want to claim Augustine's authorization for my interpretation of his meaning, I must do extensive work to grasp the precise meaning of Augustine's words (changing from one decade to the next, as we know language does)—in Latin, not in translation. I must also investigate his textual strategies, with reference to his other writings, that further reveal his perspective. This is the work of decades, if not a lifetime; it is scholars' work. But scholars are not the readers *Confessions* primarily addresses.

Augustine's Ideal Reader

"Anyone who cares to can read what I have written and interpret it as he likes" (*conf.* 9. 12). The invitation is offered without qualification, but we should note that his own criterion, relentlessly pursued from the beginning of his priesthood to his death, is that everything he says must be consistent with, if not directly supported by, scripture. He seldom used his own words if a scriptural word or passage would strengthen his thought. He quoted scripture both to reinforce and to attest the truth of his thought. Scripture, Augustine said, must augment and compensate a preacher's "poorness of speech" (*doct. chr.* 4. 5).

> My father, a fundamentalist preacher, loved scripture. When he preached, his love was evident and communicable. He took

scripture literally, rejecting critical approaches of which he may have been only tangentially aware. For him, scripture was the direct word of God, dictated, word for word in the King James version. My father believed that God said what he meant, needing only the preacher's passion effectively to communicate God's meaning to a congregation.

Augustine was quite specific about the reader for whom he wrote his *Confessions*. At the most superficial level, he begged for a reader who *would not laugh* at him as he exposed the details of his personal struggle (*conf.* 6. 6, 14; 10. 12). He also asked for sympathy, for a "kind and loving" reader (*conf.* 5. 10). I imagine him thinking, as he asked for fellow pilgrims, of the friends who accompanied and supported him throughout his youth. He asked for a reader who reads for life, as he did. He will be understood, he said, only by a reader who has *longings* (*desiderium;* ps. 122. 2; ps. 37. 4); one who is capable of "catching fire"; one who *feels* strongly; one who weeps; one who is grateful; one who is capable of feeling delight. In a late homily, St. Augustine revealed the most important criterion of all for understanding him:

> Give me a lover; that one will understand what I am saying. Give me one who desires, one who hungers, give me one who wanders in this exile and thirsts, one who sighs for the fountain of the eternal homeland, give me such a one and that one knows what I say. But if I speak to one whose heart is cold, that one is ignorant of what I am saying.
>
> (*Io.eu. tr.* 26. 4)

2

Augustine's *Coniugium*

A close reading of *Confessions* (c. 397–400), *De bono coniugali* (*The Good of Marriage*, c. 401), and *De nuptiis et concupiscentia* (*Marriage and Concupiscence*, after 418 CE) informs this chapter's discussion of the little-noticed fact that Augustine's committed relationship with his partner of fifteen years met his own later criteria for a marriage. In *De bono coniuguli*, written shortly after *Confessions*, Augustine, now a bishop, reviewed current social, ecclesiastical, and legal criteria for marriage, concluding that a sexual relationship could be called a marriage if it included the intention of faithfulness until the death of one of the partners and acceptance of children (*et potest quidem fortasse non absurd hoc appellari conubium; b. coniug.* 5. 5). His third criterion, *sacramentum*, was required for Christian marriage. When his relationship began, however, Augustine was seventeen years old; he was not a baptized Christian, nor—it is most likely—was his partner,[1] a woman "who had come my way because of my wandering desires and my lack of considered judgment" (*sedquam indagauerat uagus ardor inops prudentiae; conf.* 4. 2).

Augustine had personal experience of the sexual choices he described—except Christian marriage—from casual sex (*fornicatio*), to "adulterer at heart" (*animo adultery*), to committed relationship with the possibility of children (*coniugium*), to continence (*continentiae*). He had experienced a long marriage (by his contemporary standards), and throughout his ecclesiastical career, he discussed sexual relationships in sermons, letters, and treatises from the perspective of his own *coniugium*. He had learned that a relationship originating in *concupiscentia* must, if it is intended to be long term, mature into love: "as lust diminishes, love increases" (*ep.* 157. 2. 9; *doct. chr.* 3. 10, 15–16). Clearly, Augustine described his own relationship in these words. When his partner was "torn from his side," he remembered, "my heart, which clung to her, was broken and wounded and dropping blood" (*cor ubi adhaerebat, concisum et uulneratum mihimerat et trahebat sanguinem; conf.* 4. 2). Given his frequent insistence on understanding through "his own experience," it is noteworthy, however, that he did not make this claim in relation to sexual relationships.

Lust[2]

Augustine introduced readers of his *Confessions* to his partner in the following way:

> In those years I lived with a woman who was not bound to me in lawful marriage .... Nevertheless, I had only this one woman and I was faithful to her. And with her I learned by my own experience how great a difference there is between the self-restraint of the marriage covenant which is entered into for the sake of having children and the mere pact (*pactum libinosi amoris*) between two people whose love is lustful and who do not want to have children—even though, if children are born, they compel us to love them.
>
> (*conf.* 4. 2)

A decade after his relationship ended, when he wrote *De bono coniugali*, shortly after he had revisited the relationship as he wrote his confessions, Augustine the bishop described a committed relationship that could, "without absurdity," be considered a marriage. His purpose in this treatise was not to reconsider his own relationship, but to address problems that arose repeatedly in his parish at Hippo in North Africa. Nevertheless, it seems inevitable that in doing so his own relationship was not far from his mind. Augustine ranked the relative "goods" of sexual arrangements from celibacy,[3] which Augustine considered the greatest good, to Christian marriage, to committed relationship, the least good—but nevertheless, still a good. It is possible, he concluded, that even if the partners are legally unmarried, if their intent is to be faithful for life, and if they do not prevent the birth of children, they have a true marriage.

Augustine and his partner could claim two of the three "goods" of marriage, fidelity, and procreation; they lacked *sacramentum*. It will never be known whether they intended lifelong partnership; the duration of *any* relationship can only be *intended*. I see no reason to doubt Augustine's report that he was faithful,[4] determined as he was in writing his confessions to confess both "the bad and the good that I did" (*retr.* 2. 6). The relationship also included the birth of a child in its first year; apparently the couple did not use any of the available ways to avoid or interrupt that pregnancy. When they parted, after a temporary lapse on Augustine's part, both partners chose celibacy for the rest of their lives.

Neither happiness nor sexual compatibility was the goal of marriage in Augustine's location and social niche. At the time of his relationship, sex and legal marriage were dissociated in his mind. Instead, marriage was strongly associated in his mind with worldly success, while sex was, in his words, "abundantly available" (*conf.* 8. 7). Augustine had intelligence and ambition, but he lacked the resources and connections that a bride could offer. A wealthy and well-connected wife would have been of substantial help to an upwardly mobile young man from "the provinces."

In his early thirties, when a suitable marriage was found for him, the girl was too young for marriage.[5] According to Augustine, his mother both persuaded him of his need to marry and chose the child/woman for him. His only comment: "I liked the girl and was prepared to wait." His idea of "waiting," however, was quickly to find another woman, "not as a wife," since "I was not so much a lover of marriage as a slave to lust" (*non amator coniugii sed libidinis seruus eram; conf.* 6. 13). Augustine the bishop called a man who seeks an interim affair until a marriage could be consummated an adulterer at heart (*b. coniug.* 5).

Love

Augustine reported that his partner returned to Africa vowing that she would never "go to bed" (translator's euphemism) with another man. He admired her decision, but was unable to emulate it (*conf.* 6. 15). Readers have sometimes interpreted her choice to suggest that she was Christian. She could rather have been following a long tradition in Roman society that honors the one-man woman (*uniuira*). Augustine was grief-stricken at her loss, and he described his mourning for her in vivid and violent language. He never again undertook a committed sexual relationship.

I suspect that Augustine learned "by his own experience" that despite the best intentions of lovers, love does not always—as the saying goes—conquer all. Rather "all" often conquers love: the cooling of sexual passion, interference of family and friends, circumstances, social expectations, and human fallibility. Even before his own conversion to celibacy Augustine, astute observer of his parents' marriage, had become disenchanted with marriage. He was excited to hear of women and men who had recently converted to celibacy. Shortly after his own conversion to celibacy, he returned to Africa and founded a monastery in Hippo.

When his partner returned to Africa, however, Augustine was unprepared for the extreme devastation he experienced. The wound, created when his partner was "torn from his side," did not heal. "It burned, it hurt intensely, and then it festered, and if the pain became duller, it became more desperate" (*conf.* 6. 13). He panicked and found another lover, supposedly until the child to whom he was espoused was old enough to marry. Later, as a bishop he railed against relationships based solely on sexual gratification (*fornicatio*). He never wrote explicitly about his interim lover. He recalled his experience, however, when as a bishop he instructed others.

After Augustine's last brief affair, both he and his longtime partner lived as vowed celibates for the rest of their lives. Their celibacy, although vowed to God, perhaps also incorporated a soupçon of loyalty to one another. Why did Augustine never entertain Christian marriage as a possibility? At several points in his narrative, Augustine stated that marriage was irrevocably linked in his mind with "worldly ambition." His conversion to celibacy meant that: "I no longer sought a wife or any other worldly hope" (*conf.* 9. 1).

His conversion to celibacy brought resolution to his painfully split will (*uoluntas; conf.* 8. 10). His divided will yielded to a strongly unified feeling (*aectus*), a feeling of sweetness (*suauis*) and pleasure (*uoluptate dolcior*).

How glad I was to give up the things I had been so afraid to lose! For you cast them out from me, you true and supreme *sweetness* ... This was what you did! ... you cast them out and you entered in to me to take their place, *sweeter than all pleasure* ... Now my mind was free of those gnawing cares that came from ambition and the desire for gain and wallowing in filth and scratching the itching scab of lust.

(*libidinum; conf.* 9. 1)

Marriage

Because we know only what Augustine chose to relate about the woman with whom he lived for fifteen years, we know little about her. There may be many reasons for his reticence, but whatever these reasons were, they cannot be documented. What do we know about their relationship? Augustine's partner came to Hippo and Milan with him from North Africa. She bore a son, Adeodatus, in the first year of their cohabitation. In Roman society, children born of a concubine belonged to the mother and carried her name (Rousselle, 1988: 91). No other children were born in the following thirteen years, prompting historians to conjecture that Augustine and his partner used some form of birth control.[6] The relationship ended when Augustine and his mother identified a suitably advantageous marriage for him. The woman with whom he had lived for fifteen years returned to her home in Africa.[7] Her feeling as she departed alone, leaving their child with Augustine, can only be imagined.

Augustine's Memories

Confessions provides many examples of reconsidering, reliving, revaluing, and *repurposing* his memories. There is, for example, a considerable disparity between his fond recollections of his mother, his friends, and what he chose to reveal about his partner. The stories and sweet memories of friends, woven throughout his narrative, are conspicuously absent for his longtime partner. Even the jealous infant at the breast, perhaps his son (*conf.* 1. 7), received more of Augustine's attentive observation and comment than did his partner.

Augustine's partner is absent in his text between the occasion of their encounter until her departure to Africa. Augustine's silence regarding his partner is strikingly uncharacteristic of his memories of others. He apparently enjoyed recalling and relating incidents in the lives of his mother and his friends: Alypius, colosseum enthusiast in his youth, later bishop of Tagaste; Monica, child "drunkard," later, marathon weeper for his salvation; even the "subverters" have a place in his story, unruly students who annoyed him so much that he moved to Milan, hoping to find more orderly students (*conf.* 5. 8). No one seems to have sued him for telling their embarrassing stories! Myriad such incidents, fondly recounted, enliven *Confessions*. But there are no stories that would help his readers to picture the temperament, habits, beliefs, affections, or personality of his partner.

In the context of his many tales, it is remarkable that he did not volunteer even one small story about his partner. Readers must question such an atypical omission, observing not only what the text says, but also what is *not* to be found there—and why. This textual imbalance reveals that when he wrote his confessions he did not consider his life with her part of his inclusive cover story of God's pervasive leading. Even a narrative so extensive as to include "both the bad and the good that I did" could not, it seems, consider her role in his saga.

He appears to have categorized his life with her as part of his chaotic pursuit of elusive satisfaction, not a "story" at all—rather an unorganized, haphazard, random clutching at everything that crossed his path in the fear that something would be missed. In Augustine's master narrative, she is not so much as a "moment" in God's relentless pursuit of Augustine. Thus he placed his life with her on the almost invisible periphery of his narrative—acknowledged but not described in his chosen story. It was quite uncharacteristic of Augustine to have learned nothing from fifteen years in which he was a husband. Yet Augustine relates no incidents from his life with her between finding her, an outlet for his "wandering desires," and her return to Africa, banished from his life.

Even his violent grief at her loss tells us nothing about her or their life together; it is Augustine's story. Yet his grief, together with his alleged faithfulness, is strong evidence of his love for her: his heart was "broken, wounded, and dripping blood" when they parted. Nevertheless, lest readers conclude that he loved her dearly, in the same paragraph he hastily reinterprets. His grief at her loss, he wrote, was due to the fact that he was the "slave of an unbreakable habit" (*conf.* 6. 15). As if providing documentation for this explanation, he reported that he soon found another woman to "tide him over" until his child bride was old enough for marriage. Having *almost* acknowledged great love, he quickly recovered his project of presenting his life with his partner as *nothing but* part of a long and unhappy struggle toward celibacy.

Clearly, Augustine did not tell his readers all he had learned from his long *coniugium*. The only alternative to accepting his often reiterated explanation of "hard slavery" to sex is that their relationship must remain mysterious. He acknowledged that his grief did not fade quickly: "Nor was the wound healed which had been made by the cutting away of my former mistress. It burned, it hurt intensely, and then it festered, and if the pain became duller, it became more desperate" (*conf.* 6. 15). Can a man of Augustine's capacity to be "on fire" have been faithful to a woman for so long, and suffer so painfully at her loss, unless he loved her deeply?

Augustine even excludes her (textually) from giving birth to their child. He introduced Adeodatus, as "son of my flesh ... begotten by me in my sin ... I myself had no part in the boy except for the sin" (*ex me natum carnaliter de peccato meo; conf.* 9. 6). An odd way, indeed, to describe a beloved son, but congruent with his story. Nevertheless, he admired the boy's God-given and awe-inspiring intelligence, his childhood cleverness, and his humility.

In *Confessions*, ambivalence about his intimate relationships sometimes bleeds through the story he intends to tell. Did he think of his *coniugium* as he wrote, even as he wrote the "official" version for his ideal readers, God and "the brethren?" Did a rogue impulse stir Augustine to remember with fondness, for a moment, not only his own experience, but also the woman with whom he shared (unacknowledged) pleasure, parenthood, and everyday conversation?

Hans-Georg Gadamer wrote, "A person who seeks to understand must question what lies behind what is said" (Gadamer, 1975: 310). When Augustine wrote *Confessions* in early middle age, was his relationship still dangerous memories, threatening his celibate stability? Had he written his memoirs at a later time, would he have been able to include his partner and his experience with her with gratitude in his narrative of God's infallible leading? These possibilities can be raised only as questions; there is little evidence for raising them as suggestions.

Augustine's relationship with his longtime companion, partner, and lover was a journey in which his feeling for her transmogrified from lust to love. Readers are not told whether, during their relationship, they whispered promises of lifelong fidelity to each other. Lacking either a public ceremony or Augustine's word on the question, we must choose to offer—or not—the benefit of the doubt about what could only have been a private promise. Perhaps Augustine considered that his story of God's leading must be not so much "accurate" as deeply, profoundly *true*? This question will be considered in Chapter 5 in relation to the role of memory in Augustine's practice of meditation.

Augustine the Bishop

Given what we can know of sexual politics and practices in North Africa in the beginning years of the fifth century, a so-called double standard was socially acceptable and virtually unquestioned— except by Augustine.[8] As a bishop, Augustine was responsible for requiring Christian sexual behavior of his congregation,[9] but his authority was undermined by both Roman law and custom. The law permitted divorce; it also permitted married men to keep concubines; the church "strictly forbade" both (Meer, 1961: 181).

In *Confessions* and other writings, Augustine repeatedly invoked his "own experience" to support his understanding of an event or a scriptural quotation. It is noteworthy that he did not do so when, as a bishop, he discussed sexual practices in two treatises, *De bono coniugali* and *De sancta uirginitate* (*On Holy Virginity*). Nevertheless, he was not reluctant to exercise his authority: he instructed wives to be jealous of their husbands; in a sermon he inveighed, "I order it. I command it. Your bishop commands it. And Christ commands it through me" (*s.* 392. 3; Meer, 1961: 182). In *Confessions*, Augustine had expressed admiration for Monica's skill in not seeing what she was not "supposed" to see in the behavior of her unfaithful husband. She also taught other women to serve their husbands as slaves, ignoring "their master's" behavior (*conf.* 9. 9).

However, the bishop's sermons scold wives for just such "blindness" (*s.* 392. 4, 5; *s.* 332. 4).

He was no less adamant in requiring of men marital fidelity. To a chorus of loud complaints, Augustine informed men, "Any woman who sleeps with you other than your wife is a prostitute." He was forceful in instructing wives not to withhold sex from their husbands, even for religious reasons and for temporary periods. To do so, he insisted, is tantamount to *inviting* a man to resort to a concubine or prostitute.

Memories of his own *coniugium* inevitably crept into his instructions to others. Although in *Confessions*, he gave his partner short shrift, indicating his inability to understand her role as part of his governing narrative of God's leading in his life, *De bono coniugali* exposes a subtle change in his thinking. His suggestion that even lacking *sacramentum*, a committed relationship that did not prevent the birth of children can be considered a true marriage represented a surreptitious revision and revaluing of his own *coniugium* years.

Interpreting Augustine

Reading for life, through the lens of a thirty-four-year marriage, I recognize my experience in Augustine's insightful comment on the inevitable evolution of a good marriage: "In proportion as the dominion of *concupiscentia is pulled down, in the same proportion that of love is built up*" (*doct. chr.* 3. 10; emphasis added). This observation incisively grasps "the good of marriage." The startling difference between Augustine's first encounter with his lover, motivated by his "wandering desires and lack of considered judgment," and their parting, in which his heart "clung to her, broken," reveals the pattern of their long relationship, namely, the slow decline of lust and steady increase of love. Augustine's grief at the loss of his partner indicates that his love for her had grown exponentially since the early days of their relationship.

Moreover, nothing stabilizes a marriage more effectively than the birth of a child. A woman's body rather quickly changes from a sexual body to a working body. Long before the 'labor' of childbirth occurs, nausea, bodily changes, and increasing discomfort demand of both partners a different kind of attentiveness to her body. Even when a child is fervently desired, pregnancy changes a relationship. The birth of the child solidifies that change, as the needs of a helpless and loudly demanding infant take precedence over those of its parents.

After long experience with another person, one comes to know—and to love—the other as a human being with loveable qualities, yes, but also faults, fears, and weaknesses. Released at last from "enslavement" to society's repeatedly reiterated scenario for "falling in love," we may be able to begin to see the other as a suffering and struggling human being rather than as a socially designated sex object. The relationship depends precariously on the timetable of this adjustment. One partner may be slower than the other to accept the diminishment of lust and to notice and enjoy the increments of love. If the balance between lust and love becomes radically different, the partner who requires that lust define the relationship is likely to seek other *concupiscentia*-saturated encounters. If this occurs the marriage suffers, often terminally.

Original Sin

Did Augustine's sexual experience inform his most notorious and contentious doctrine, the doctrine of original sin? Augustine noticed himself with a seriousness and profundity unmatched by any author of his time. "My personal experience enabled me to understand ... I knew from my own experience" (*conf.* 7. 16; 8. 5). I suggest that the Christian version of original sin articulated by Augustine is founded, not primarily on Augustine's experience, but on his effort to understand his experience. Having reached an explanation that satisfied him, he then considered his experience *universal*, projecting that explanation onto every member of the human race.

The concept of original sin was not new. In Judaism and earlier Christianity, original sin named a vague presentiment that something is not quite *right* about human nature. Two centuries earlier, Augustine's fellow North African, Tertullian, had named this undertow of human life "weakness" (*uitium*). Augustine's youthful experience required a much darker, more pervasive, and profound taint; he named it "sin" (*peccatum*). His next move was decisive: he said that original sin was a *feeling*, *concupiscentia*—*lust* —and this well-nigh universal feeling is the evidence, the *proof*, of original sin. In Augustine's vivid description, an abstract idea—original sin—"collapsed into immediacy," becoming experiential, even performative.

Augustine soldered lust to original sin, a conceptual move that was both brilliant and damaging: brilliant, because it escalated a nagging intimation of inadequacy into a virtually universal feeling; damaging, for generations who inherited the practical and institutional effects of his pervasive authority. Lust, a component of the collection of emotions, intellect, memories, and intentions that comprise human feeling (discussed in Chapter 1), is strong enough to split feeling into warring attractions, in precisely the way that Augustine described in *Confessions* as a "divided will."

In his late contentious correspondence with Iulian, exiled Pelagian Bishop of Eclanum, Augustine insisted that children do not inherit their Christian parents' faith, but are born as the devil's property; to become established as God's children, they must be baptized. Augustine himself was baptized on his own initiative, as an adult. He understood his mother's rationale for not having him baptized as a child or youth—something about letting him "get it out of his system"—but he thought later that he would have been helped by baptism in childhood. He was, he says, a believer as a youth; he had already begun to reject philosophies and beliefs that omitted the name of Christ.

Expounding his understanding of original sin, Augustine realized that he was in danger of being accused of entertaining the Manichaean doctrine of two *natures*. Manichaean theology taught that in every human being there is a good and an evil nature, awkwardly stuck together and perpetually warring. To differentiate his teaching from that of Manichaeans, he specified firmly that the "divided will" is not two wills, but he *himself*: "It was 'I' who willed it and I who was unwilling. It was the same I throughout" (*ego eram, qui non uolebam; ego qui uolebam … mecum contendebam et dissipabar a me ipso*). Because a person can be attracted to many objects of desire, many fragments of will—not just two—may be in conflict in the same person. When desire "is not total and complete … it is torn apart and heavily distressed as truth puts one way first and habit will not allow the other way to be abandoned" (*dum illus ueritate praeponent, hoc familiaritate non point; conf.* 8. 10).

There were immediate objections to Augustine's intensification of original sin from a hazy presentiment into a sexual feeling. First, Augustine's experience of sexuality was not as universal as he thought. Iulian of Eclanum, for one, had not experienced Augustine's rambunctious sexuality. He argued that the sexual urge was God-given, both for human pleasure and—obviously—for the continuation of the human race. Sexual activity, like any other pleasure, Iulian conceded, must be monitored and disciplined, but he saw no problem in confining its expression to Christian marriage.

Second, and still considering possible effects of Augustine's sexual experience on his most characteristic doctrine: Augustine used a gender-specific illustration and defense for a doctrine for which he claimed universality, thus revealing its foundation in, and limitation to, his "own experience." Noticing the physical operation of his own *concupiscentia*, he did not pause to notice that women's bodies function differently. He stated that the sexual act cannot occur without involuntary "motion ... of the members of the body expressly created for this purpose" (*nupt. et conc.* 7). The insubordinate "disobedience" of the sexual members (which do not always obey will's instructions) demonstrated to Augustine that Adam's disobedience to God continues to be reenacted in male sexual organs' insubordination to the will. It was impotence, not sex, which fascinated Augustine (*ciu.* 14. 16). Discussing the rape of Roman women in the 410 CE Sack of Rome, he made the insidious suggestion that "perhaps" rape could not "have been undergone without some bodily pleasure" (*ciu.* 1. 16). Had he listened to the account of a raped woman, he could not have made this ill-advised comment.

Can the unconscious universalization of one's own experience be avoided? Certainly, we know the world by projection, but at what point do our projections become misleading, counter-productive, or dangerous? At his most recollected Augustine would urge, I think, the importance of humility in our inevitably perspectival interpretations. Just because one has experienced something does not necessarily mean that it illuminates something about the world and everyone else. One who reads "for life" must be prepared respectfully to entertain opposing interpretations, each based on experience. If Augustine's exhortations to humility—"firstly humility, secondly humility, and thirdly humility" *ep.* 118. 3)—had become a priority in the history of the Christian traditions—necessarily, however, at the cost of other allegiances, such as scripture, tradition, and authority, even "experience"—the history of Christian theology would be very different.

3

Augustine's Conversions

"So much depends on how we understand what happened to us. So much depends on how we tell ourselves the story of our lives" (Gaines, 1998: 38). *Confessions*, Augustine "telling himself the story of his life," narrated many conversions in which a settled opinion, belief, or practice was challenged, shown to be an impediment, and abandoned. His journey toward "Wisdom" gathered momentum and urgency when he read Cicero's *Hortensius* at the age of nineteen, but he recognized that it began in earliest childhood, "at that time I already believed" (*conf.* 1. 11), and continued through his youth and beyond. Each of these conversions involved not only awareness of the limitation or falseness of the old perspective, but also recognition and adoption of a more accurate and productive attitude or belief. Each also required the "collapse" of new understanding into the "immediacy" of his life, altering, as he noted repeatedly, his "way of *feeling*."

When did Augustine's conversion to Christianity occur? Many readers would say that it coincided with his conversion to celibacy. By his own report, sexuality was an especially vexing problem, a problem over which he said he had no control. Certainly, he gave this conversion a great deal of literary attention—a detailed background, vivid description, and a permanent resolution—all signals of its importance. I do not seek to diminish its significance; it should, however, be framed within two important considerations.

First, Augustine lived in an historical moment in which there was a virtual frenzy for asceticism in the Christian Roman Empire. During the fourth century, Christianity had changed from a heavily persecuted sect at the beginning of the century, to the official religion of the empire by the last decade of the century. The change could not have been more dramatic. In the first decade, the

Diocletian persecution claimed several thousand Christian martyrs, the highest number for a single persecution in the history of the western empire. By the end of the century, traditional Roman religions were suppressed, magnificent state-funded cathedrals were built, Jews were excluded from public office, and synagogues destroyed; dissident Christians were punished or exiled. Not all Christians were pleased with the new legitimacy and state support. Dissent frequently took the form of asceticism, especially sexual asceticism. Iovinian was the only fifth-century Christian theologian who claimed that marriage was equal with celibacy as a condition in which a Christian life can be conducted. Augustine called Iovinian a "monster" (*retr.* 2. 48. 1). In brief, Augustine's conversion to celibacy occurred in the social context of passionate Christian interest in sexual asceticism.

Second, Augustine's conversion to celibacy ought to be enclosed in the more capacious framework of his life which was, in fact, the format in which he discussed it. It was *part* of his process of becoming Christian that included many less sensational conversions. It is the long *process* itself that should be understood as Augustine's conversion to Christianity. It included: conversion from the Academics' despair of finding truth to acceptance of the legitimacy of belief (*conf.* 5. 10; 6. 4–5; 6. 11),[1] conversion to the authority of scripture (*conf.* 3. 5; 6. 5; 6. 11, 7. 21); conversion to an incorporeal spiritual universe (*conf.* 5. 14; 6. 3; 7. 14; 7. 17; 7. 20; 8. 1); conversion from pride to humility (*conf.* 7. 18; 7. 20); conversion to interiority/subjectivity (*conf.* 7. 7; 9. 4; 12. 16), to the Catholic Church (*conf.* 6. 4–5), renunciation of worldly ambition (*conf.* 8. 1; 8. 5); and conversion to celibacy (*conf.* 8. 12). Other conversions followed. For example, he dramatically revised his esteem for his rhetorical training, described judgmentally in *Confessions* as merely a route to worldly success (*doct. chr.* 4. 2). Each of the conversions Augustine described deserves a closer look. None stands alone; each requires and integrates former conversions and paves the way for those to follow.

Unhappiness

Both Augustine and Freud, many centuries later, described personal unhappiness as a prerequisite for seeking fundamental change

(Miles, "Self Deception," 2012: 115–30). A person who is happy *enough* will not change. Augustine was excruciatingly aware of his unhappiness, as were Freud's patients who underwent the difficult and labor-intensive process of psychoanalysis.

Augustine had education and a successful career as a teacher of rhetoric, but his unhappiness was not alleviated by these achievements. "How unhappy I was then, and you [God] made me really see my unhappiness!" Rather than easing his unhappiness, he wrote, God increased it. His images are startlingly physical: "You pricked my wound on its quick" (*conf.* 4. 6; 6. 6); "You were breaking my bones with the rod of your discipline" (*conf.* 9. 1). He declared his unhappiness repeatedly, metaphors piling on metaphors, on page after page of *Confessions*. He wrote of "goads and stings," of a starving mind, lacking real nourishment, that "goes licking at shadows" (*conf.* 4. 6; 6. 6), and of chains and hard slavery (*conf.* 8. 7). Augustine was vividly, deeply (and very articulately) unhappy.

Attributing physical pain and emotional anguish to God, as Augustine frequently did in his *Confessions,* appears to be contradictory to later theological statements in which he stated that God does not punish sinners, for God does not visit evil on anyone. Sinners are punished, rather, by the inevitable *effects* of their sins: "When God punishes sinners he does not inflict on them his evil, but abandons them to their own evils" (*ps.* 5. 10). Punishment, he said, occurs "by necessary connections" (*necessitatibus distributae; solil.* 1. 1. 4). In other words, sin is its own worst punishment. Yet when describing the collapse of abstract theology into the immediacy of his own life, Augustine experienced and described what he *felt,* namely God's direct punishment: "You were breaking my bones …." His alternative descriptions of sin and its effects, although apparently contradictory, are simply two perspectives on the same phenomena, one abstractly theological, the other acutely personal. Both are true.

Conversions

Augustine's youthful search for certainty began with the intellectual's anguished question, "Where can I find the books?" (*conf.* 6. 11). He was initially attracted by the Academics' "certain uncertainty";

their teaching that everything was doubtable seemed to provide a certainty that was better than none. However, he quickly found that even this "certainty" proved inadequate; it offered no guidance for his life. "No, it cannot be," he said; "we must look into things more carefully and not give up hope" (*conf.* 5. 10). He soon recognized that the Academics' dogmatic uncertainty was itself a belief. Each of Augustine's subsequent conversions depended on his realization that belief, scorned (but practiced) by the Academics, was a legitimate option. But which belief? Undecided, he determined to "take my stand where my parents placed me as a child until I can see the truth plainly." From this vantage point, he said, "It is not for nothing; it is not meaningless that all over the world is displayed the high and towering authority of the Christian faith." He concluded, for the moment, that he would "prefer the Christian faith" (*conf.* 6. 5; 7. 7), and he became a catechumen (*conf.* 6. 11).

The frustration Augustine experienced with the "truths" on offer prepared him for one of his most important conversions, namely, conversion to the authority of scripture. "Those things in the scripture which used to seem absurd are not absurd; they can be understood in a different and perfectly good way" (*conf.* 6. 11). "I therefore decided to give my attention to the study of the Holy Scriptures and to see what they were like .... And what I saw was something that is not discovered by the proud ... the way in is low and humble, but inside the vault is high and veiled in mysteries" (*conf.* 3. 5).

Augustine was still impeded in his effort to find truth by his inability to imagine an incorporeal spiritual universe: "If only I had been able to form the idea of a substance that was spiritual" (*conf.* 5. 14). He sighed in retrospect, "I was unable to form an idea of any kind of substance other than what my eyes were accustomed to see." Because he had read that human beings were made in God's image, he struggled to imagine God in humans' image, that is, in a body that would "fill the infinite distances of all space" (*conf.* 7. 1). He was relieved, however, to find that he had confused the allegations of the Church's critics with the teachings of the Church.

> I was both confounded and converted (*conuertebar*), and I was glad, my God, that your only Church, the body of your only son—that Church in which the name of Christ had been put upon

me as an infant—was not flavored with this childish nonsense and did not, in her healthy doctrine, maintain the view that you, the creator of all things, could be in the form of a human body, packed into a definite space which, however mighty and large, must still be bounded on all sides.

(conf. 6. 4)

Augustine narrated this important conversion to a subjective spiritual universe *twice*. First, he described it according to the cover story of his life; he went to sleep, he wrote, and God did it.

You laid your kindly hand upon my head and covered up my eyes so that they should not see vanity, and then I relaxed a little from myself (*cessaui de me paululum*) and sleep fell upon my madness. And I woke up in you and saw you infinite in a different way.

(conf. 7. 14)

Yet, a few chapters later, he said that it was his reading of "the Platonists' books" that "taught me to see a truth that was incorporeal" (*conf.* 7. 20). In this account, Augustine said that he finally understood, thanks to reading the right books.

Why did Augustine offer two explanations of how he came to understand the existence of a spiritual universe? Which one is accurate? Most twenty-first century-readers would probably think that the accurate version is that Augustine read a lot, thought a lot, and figured it out. However, interpreted in this way, God's leading goes unacknowledged; but Augustine had no story other than God's leading into which to fit this momentous experience. Any incident or experience that fell outside the story of God's intimate and continuous leading was disorganized, haphazard, "scattered and spilled" (*conf.* 11. 29), "scattered fragments" (*conf.* 2. 1). Lacking the narrative of God's leading, there is *no story*, only flailing limbs, the "inmost bowels of [his] heart torn apart with the crowding tumults of variety" and "scratching the itching scab of concupiscence" (*conf.* 9. 1)—not a pretty picture, nothing but random acts, accidental events, and self-loathing.

On the other hand, Augustine's "laundered memories," discussed in Chapter 4, tell a coherent story. His first explanation of how he came to understand the existence of a spiritual universe was God's leading. *This* story was the *truth* of his life, even though the second account may also be *accurate*. He attempted to integrate the two accounts, speculating that the *timing* of his reading of the Platonic authors was part of God's plan. Had he read them at a later time, he supposed, the result could have been quite different. The *precision* of God's operation in his life was remarkable and convincing to him. In his chosen story, God was "dragging me by the force of my own desires," toward an as-yet barely discernable goal. "I ceased to have any doubt that there was an incorruptible substance from which came every substance" (*conf.* 8. 1).

Augustine's conversions accumulate, building on one another. Next, Augustine understood that he saw truthfully only when he recognized "the *way* to you (God) in Christ our Savior." At this moment, he converted to the fundamental importance of humility: "Humility was not a subject those [Platonist] books would ever have taught me." The difference between *seeing the goal* and *seeing the way* is the difference between (abstract) intellectual understanding and "living there," immediacy (*conf.* 7. 20, 21). Humility made the difference between understanding the theology and "walking the walk." The way of humility was exemplified by Jesus Christ: "the Word was made flesh and dwelt among men" (*conf.* 7. 9).

Augustine was convinced intellectually of the critical importance of humility, yet he resisted this conversion for some time:

> I was not humble enough to possess Jesus in his humility as my God, nor did I know what lesson was taught by his weakness .... He built for himself a humble dwelling out of our clay ... healing the swelling of our pride, and fostering our love, so that ... [we] should put on weakness, seeing divinity in the weakness that it had put on by wearing our "coat of skin."
>
> (*conf.* 7. 18)

The difference between the two narratives of Augustine's conversion to a spiritual universe lies in the different *feeling* of each. Both narratives describe the same intellectual understanding, namely, the existence of a spiritual universe, but the *feeling* is different. The feeling of pride is self-importance: "I had begun to want to have the reputation of a wise man ... I was puffed up with my knowledge." The feeling of humility is weakness (*infirmus*), leading to gratitude for help. Augustine could never recommend highly enough the virtue of humility. His hostility to pride might be summarized: "The proud cannot find you" (*conf.* 5. 2).

Augustine's difficulty in trying to imagine an incorporeal universe that his "eyes cannot see" was complicated by his initial lack of understanding that the spiritual universe is accessible only to interiority or subjectivity. Again, reading books by "the Platonists," Augustine was "admonished to return to my own self and enter into the innermost part of myself." He described his conversion to interiority as one of his more spectacular conversions, a sound and light spectacle: "You beat back the weakness of my sight, blazing upon me with your rays"; he saw an "unchangeable light (not the ordinary light) shining above the eye of my soul and my mind." "And I heard," he continued, "as one hears things with the heart, [and] would sooner have doubted my own life than the existence of that truth" (*conf.* 7. 10). Augustine invoked physical senses to describe interior senses. He saw with "the eye of the soul," and heard "with the ear of the heart."

> You were within me and I was outside, and there I sought for you and in my ugliness I plunged into the beauties you have made. You were with me, and I was not with you (*ecce intus eras et ego foris*) …. You called, you cried out, you shattered my deafness; you flashed, you shone, you scattered my blindness; you breathed perfume, and I drew in my breath and I pant for you; I tasted, and I am hungry and thirsty; you touched me, and I burned for your peace.
>
> (*conf.* 10. 27)

After his conversion to interiority, he was frustrated in his attempts to communicate the experience to others: "If only they could see the eternal light inside themselves, [but] their hearts look out of their eyes away from you" (*conf.* 9. 4).

The inter*connection* between Augustine's conversions is evident. One conversion both enabled and required the next. Weaving his cover story through the thoughts, incidents, and feeling at the moments of his life, he narrated God's activity in his life. In retrospect, no incident, no frustration, no question was accidental or coincidental. Each was essential, converging in his conversion from "marriage and worldly success" to celibacy.

Augustine's Prototypes of Conversion: Reading

With what patterns of conversion was Augustine familiar? Introducing his conversion to celibacy, he related several conversions he had recently heard of for the first time. In visits with Simplicianus, Victorinus, and Ponticianus, he was told of both earlier and contemporary conversions. More than a century earlier, St. Antony, an Egyptian monk and the prototypical ascetic, heard the words of the gospel, "Go, sell all you have, give to the poor ... and follow me." Renouncing his family's wealth, Antony obeyed immediately (*conf.* 8. 6). Simplicianus told Augustine of the conversion of Victorinus, a learned man whose statue stood in the Roman forum. Victorinus had believed in Christ privately, but Simplicianus urged him to consent to the "humility" of baptism and a public declaration of his faith. Hearing his story, Augustine was "on fire to be like him" (*exarsi imitandum; conf.* 8. 5). The experience of being "on fire" on hearing of another's conversion was a prologue to his own. What struck Augustine was the *affective* quality of these stories rather than their *intellectual* content.

Ponticianus had another story to tell: he was walking with several friends who were officials in the emperor's civil service when two of them found a book about St. Antony in a house along the way. They began to read and were transfixed. Augustine compared the extremity of emotion experienced by the readers to that of giving birth. The two men immediately decided to emulate Antony. Joined by the women to whom they were engaged, they resolved to "dedicate their virginity" to God (*conf.* 8. 6). Excited by these current examples of conviction and sacrifice, Augustine entered the fierce battle with himself that led to his conversion to celibacy.

Elements of these conversion stories recur in Augustine's own narrative. First, these conversions were prompted by reading experiences. Each was precipitated by a biblical text that was "heard" as speaking directly to the lives of its readers; each produced a sudden overpowering change of feeling. Similarly, Augustine's conversion included reading a scripture verse that carried the immediacy of a direct command (Romans 13:13-14). Second, the sacrifice of a highly valued good was involved in each conversion: Antony relinquished wealth; Victorinus surrendered his public image; and Ponticianus's friends and their fiancés forfeited sex and worldly success, as did Augustine.

Just as readers of the *Confessions* have focused attention on Augustine's dramatic conversion to celibacy, overlooking the incremental conversions by which he became Christian, his repudiation of worldly ambition has received scant attention. Perhaps this is because he quickly became influential in a new field of opportunity and upward mobility at the end of the fourth century, namely, the Christian Church. Because Augustine's readers know the outcome of his resolution, we do not recognize the "weight" of this sacrifice of his childhood ambition. At the time, however, Augustine renounced worldly success without knowing what he forfeited.

Conversion to Celibacy, Preamble

Augustine, middle-aged author of the *Confessions*, seemed reluctant to recall and relive the passion and pain of his youthful conversion to celibacy. He repeatedly postponed re-experiencing the fervid feeling of his memories, suddenly alighting, apparently with relief, on a topic by which he can delay further. First he rehearsed the long background of the present moment, from infancy, when he imbibed with his mother's milk the "still deeply cherished" name of Christ, to his incandescent enthusiasm for the pursuit of wisdom as a youth. Recalling his lengthy pilgrimage, he marveled that he had been stuck for so long, had made so little progress. Pausing to deplore his hesitation to commit to Christ's service he wrote, astonished: "At least twelve years have gone by since I was nineteen and reading Cicero, fired with an enthusiasm for wisdom, yet I was still putting off the moment!" (*conf*. 8. 7).

He delayed to recall the friends who were also an important feature of his developing story: the "unfriendly friends" (*inimical amacitia conf*. 2. 9) with whom he stole pears as a boy; mutually exploitive friends, "eating each other up as people do with their food" (*sicut cibum assolet, amando consumentem conf*. 9. 2); and companions of early adulthood who suffered and struggled alongside the volatile Augustine. In their company he had spent all his time and energy on pursuing two attachments in whose strong grip he still remained: "the bondage of my desire for sex, and my slavery to the affairs of this world" (*conf.* 8. 6). Again he named his captors: "the treasures and kingdoms of men [and] the pleasures of the body easily and abundantly available" (*conf.* 8. 7).

Remembering in detail the events and people along his journey may seem to his readers unnecessary and frustrating postponements of his story. But these events and people are the details that support his demonstration of God's leading. Re-telling these memories, he *gathered* the experiences by which he was led to the moment.

Augustine's narrative of his conversion to celibacy is an extended analysis of feeling. In the prolonged preamble to this story, he paused the stream of his narrative to discuss several general questions about feeling. Why is it that "the more pain there is first, the more joy there is after?" Why is joy exponentially greater when shared by a number of people (*conf.* 8. 3; 8. 2)? These topics seem irrelevant as an introduction to his conversion to celibacy. In fact, they disappeared, unresolved, as his emotions gripped him.

But Augustine is *still* not ready. Once again he breaks the flow of his narrative, postponing the moment of reentering the emotional violence of this conversion, by exploring the dilemma of the "two wills." This was the quandary which froze his decision to accept the Christian life, the decision that would, he believed, require him to repudiate both worldly success and sexual pleasure. "All I had to do was to will to go there, and I would not only go but would immediately arrive," but his locked wills detained him, "turning and twisting this way and that ... half maimed, struggling ... the will to do and the power to do are not the same thing" (*conf.* 8. 9).

As Augustine learned, will is not the servant of reason. He proposed no philosophical arguments for the choices he faced, either for marriage or for celibacy. Except for citing the Apostle Paul's stated preference for celibacy, he presented no argument from scripture or Christian doctrine. Augustine's identification of "two wills" at war with one another had less to do with his *mind* "divided against itself" than it had to do with a strongly ambivalent *feeling* that he characterized as "self against self" (*ipso aduersus me ipsum; conf.* 8. 11; 5. 10). *Uoluntas,* will, wish, or inclination, is not based on intellect or reason; it is not two minds in conflict; the division occurred in his *feeling,* the powerful life-directing collection and expression of the whole person. Two irreconcilable delights attracted Augustine: on the one hand, "I can be a friend of

God *now*" (*conf.* 8. 6); on the other hand, "But wait. These worldly things too are sweet; the pleasure they give is not inconsiderable; we must not be too hasty to reject them" (*conf.* 6. 11).

Surely he can have both; neither scripture nor the Church requires his celibacy. Of course he could—*if he were a different person*. But he had experienced himself as enslaved, in "iron bondage": "From a perverse will came lust, and slavery to lust became a habit, and the habit, being constantly yielded to, became a necessity…. These were like links, hanging each to each, and they held me fast in a hard slavery" (*conf.* 8. 5). Augustine was appropriately respectful of the durability of habit. As a self-professed addict, he recognized that he could not allow himself a gift that others could enjoy with gratitude.

He was perplexed and dismayed that mind was unable to "issue an order to itself and have it obeyed," but he did not (in *Confessions*) resort to citing original sin. What we might call "will power" is precisely mind's intransigent but ineffectual effort to legislate for the whole person. Augustine called will power pride, the enemy of humility which recognizes that it needs help, and asks for it.

Conversion to Celibacy

Augustine, theologian of feeling, narrated his conversion to celibacy as a crisis of feeling in which his body expressed his strong emotions. As he was immersed in, and overwhelmed by, the mental and physical violence of his emotions, *his feeling changed*. His earlier conversions altered thoughts, perceptions, and attitudes; his conversion to celibacy was uniquely, though not solely, a conversion that intimately affected his body. His other conversions did not feature floods of tears, a writhing body, and a tortured mind. Although Augustine insisted that lust (*concupiscentia*) was not grounded in body, but in the restless mind fearful of missing any passing pleasure, sexual concupiscence, for Augustine the paradigm of all desires, was acted out in his body. The preamble to conversion was self-loathing. The imagery is physical:

> You, Lord, were turning me around so that I could see myself; you took me from behind my own back … and you set me

in front of my own face so that I could see how foul a sight I was—crooked, filthy, spotted and ulcerous (*distortus et sordidus, maculosus et ulcerosus*). I saw, and I was horrified ... I tried to look away from myself ... and again you were setting me in front of myself, forcing me to look into my own face, so that I might see my sin and hate it.

(*conf.* 8. 7)

Augustine continued: "I was gnawed at inside (*rodebar intus*) ... I was lost and overwhelmed with a terrible kind of shame." A "mute shrinking" (*muta trepidation*) gripped him, a hesitation that "feared like death to be restrained from the flux of a habit by which it was melting away into death." "My face was as perturbed as my mind." His boyhood friend, Alypius, stared at him in amazement: "My forehead, cheeks, eyes, the color of my face, and the inflection of my voice expressed my mind better than the words I used." "I was mad and dying; but there was sanity in my madness, life in my death" (*conf.* 8. 8).

Copious tears accompanied Augustine's conversion to celibacy, and his restlessness was at its most extreme. Augustine's bones "cried out"; he thrashed about, tore his hair, beat his forehead; he locked his fingers together, clasped his knee. Yet once again, he paused the narration to puzzle about the absurdity that "when the mind gives an order to the body, the order is immediately obeyed; [yet] when the mind gives an order to itself, there is resistance" (*conf.* 8. 9). Again he invoked the dilemma of the two wills—only two? no, many, he corrected himself—none of which is strong enough to deliver unified intention and action. Mind's "will power" cannot unify *feeling*, the agent of the gathered self. Arguments are useless; feeling is divided: "I fought with myself and was torn apart by myself" (*ista controversia in corde meo non nisi deme ipso aduersus me ipsum*; *conf.* 8. 11).

"Sick and in torture," the painfully conflicted Augustine is confronted by *amicae meae*—my girlfriends—who pulled at him *by his garment of flesh* (*succutiebant uestrem meam carnem; conf.* 8. 11), murmuring, "never again? ... are you *sure*?" No subtle persuasion here, rather "violence of habit." The force invoked was a *physical* as well as an emotional compulsion (*consuetudo uiolenta*).

The murmuring, coaxing, whiny voices of the girl friends were answered, in Augustine's mind, by the calm, serene, cheerful voice of Continence. She simply smiled and held out her arms to embrace him, as if to say, "Why do you try to stand by yourself, and so not stand at all? Let him support you. Do not be afraid. He will not draw away and let you fall. Put yourself fearlessly in his hands. He will receive you and will make you well" (*conf.* 8. 11). The image is of a toddler (Augustine's son, Adeodatus), taking his first trembling steps to fling himself triumphantly into his mother's trustworthy arms.

Augustine wept on. Locked in bitter struggle, both internal and physical, "himself against himself," he heard a voice that said, "Take! read!" "At once my face changed" (*conf.* 8. 12). Excited as he was, he considered whether these words belonged to some childhood game. Recalling the story of St. Antony, he decided that he must follow St. Antony's example, accepting the words as directed at him. Picking up a book of scripture lying nearby, he read: "Put on the Lord Jesus Christ and make no provision for the flesh in concupiscence." Those words collapsed into the immediacy of his life: "immediately ... my heart was filled with a light of confidence and all the shadows of my doubt were swept away." "Reading" his own body, the text that revealed his feeling, Augustine reports, "by now my face was perfectly calm." He *felt his subjective change on the skin and in the muscles of his face*. His indecision vanished; his desire for a wife and "any other worldly hope" disappeared (*conf.* 8. 12). His conversions to God's service were complete.

Friends continued to accompany Augustine: Alypius, his boyhood friend, with whom Augustine felt "in privacy" in the drama of his conversion to celibacy (*conf.* 8. 8); his son, Adeodatus, and the friends with whom he was baptized and retreated to explore the Christian faith at Cassiciacum. He acknowledged the value of a good friend: "No surer step toward God can be imagined than the love between man and man" (*mor.* 1. 26. 48).[2] Yet he did not include—much less, feature—his longtime partner among his friends. Augustine, product of his society's "river of human custom ... hellish river of custom," never called a woman a friend (*conf.* 1. 16).

Converting Body

Augustine's process of becoming Christian continued. His youthful attitude toward bodies—his own and others'—was as objects of lust:

> And so I muddied the clear spring of friendship with the dirt of physical desire and clouded over its brightness with the dark hell of lust .... It was a sweet thing to me both to love and to be loved, and more sweet still when I was able to enjoy the body of my lover.
>
> (*conf.* 3. 1)

For the young Augustine, bodies were ambiguous and volatile: at their best, they give and receive pleasure; at worst, they sicken and die (*conf.* 5. 9). As discussed in Chapter 6, his thinking concerning human bodies changed dramatically in old age.

Augustine interpreted physical pain and illness as one of God's teaching methods. As a youth he had learned that God works through bodies, even without a person's conscious intention. A friend was baptized while unconscious and expected to die. When he recovered, he took his baptism seriously, reproving Augustine severely for joking about it (*conf.* 4. 4). A painful lung constriction forced Augustine to early retirement (*conf.* 9. 3); and shortly before his baptism, "you tortured me with toothache" (*conf.* 9. 4). Augustine attributed painful experience to God's agenda of bringing him to God's purpose for his life. God "pricked the wound," "broke his bones" (*conf.* 6. 6), and administered "goads and stings." God "leveled me" (*conplanaueris,* literally "planed"), leaving Augustine scratching itching scabs, starving, and "licking at shadows" (*conf.* 9. 4). These desperate metaphors are not theological language, but vivid depictions of how his experience *felt.*

Augustine's conversion to celibacy was unique; his former conversions were provoked by changes in his intellect that created changes in his feeling. Yet none of these conversions directly confronted his *concupiscentia,* which simply carried on—business as usual—unthreatened. When his partner returned to Africa, he was desolate, but quickly found another lover, *so that* his lust was "fed and kept alive so that it might reach ... matrimony just as strong as before, or stronger, and still the slave of an unbreakable habit" (*conf.* 6. 15).

The dissident voice in his struggle toward commitment to God's service was the well-exercised strong voice of his body, immersed and strengthened in "the deep gulf of carnal pleasure" (*conf.* 6. 15, 16). Little wonder that Augustine's feeling was divided; as his ideas and beliefs focused and strengthened, so did his *embodied* resistance, acted out in his lust. The physical and emotional cataclysm he described in *Confessions* 8. 12 entailed nothing less than a gathering of his scattered fragments into the story of God's insistent and intransigent leading.

Becoming Christian

As this chapter has demonstrated, Augustine's conversion to celibacy, usually referred to simply as his "conversion," occurred within a series of conversions, both preceding and following. The result of his textual strategies, discussed above, was to divert attention from earlier conversions without which that spectacular conversion was unlikely to occur. At the time only his mother noticed "to her joy" that Augustine was coming closer every day to baptism (*conf*. 5. 13; 6. 13). At the time, Augustine himself, plagued by fears and pains, both physical and psychic, did not recognize until afterward that "I was drawing gradually nearer" (*conf*. 5. 13–14). From a later perspective he saw that each of his incremental conversions was part of God's leading, a slow development of experiences and intellectual understandings which gradually changed his "feeling," his love.[3]

However, his conversion to celibacy in *Confessions* 8. 12 is the account that became famous. Describing this conversion, Augustine again used the language of vivid sensory experience—turned up a notch—that he had used in relating earlier conversions: "You called, you cried out, you shattered my deafness: you flashed, you shone, you scattered my blindness; you breathed perfume, and I drew in my breath and I pant for you: I tasted, and I am hungry and thirsty; you touched me and I burned for your peace" (*conf*. 10. 27).

Reading Augustine

I might (vainly) wish that Augustine were not so greatly endowed with the literary skill by which his dramatic conversion to celibacy became the dominant model of Christian conversion. It did not, however, become so for centuries. Medieval monks did not report spectacular conversions. Rather, they wept quietly in meditation, adopting instead Augustine's account in *Confessions* of a long *practice and process* of conversion. Augustine was not suddenly and miraculously catapulted into *being* Christian; rather, he *became* Christian across a lifetime. Even "the apostle" (Paul), Augustine's mentor and model, repeatedly denied achievement in the Christian life. He spoke, rather, of "straining toward the goal," "pressing toward the mark," and "running hard" (*ps.* 130. 14). Augustine remarked at length on St. Paul's denial of *having arrived*:

> He says that he is not yet perfect because he has not yet received, because he has not yet laid hold ... he is stretching out ... pushing on. He is on the way; he is hungry; he wishes to be filled; he is anxious; he desires to arrive; he is passionately inflamed.
>
> (*util. ieiun.* 1)

Like Paul, Augustine saw himself as *en route*, becoming Christian, as one who, when "he cannot see you for the distance, may yet walk along the road by which he will arrive and see you and lay hold on you" (*conf.* 7. 21).

Augustine's dramatic conversion to celibacy was not considered normative for Christian conversion until the sixteenth century, when a crisis of religious authority created new respect for individual experience. Describing their own sensational conversions, religious leaders such as Martin Luther, John Bunyan, and John Wesley inspired copycat conversion experiences. Foreshortened for dramatic effect, these conversions included long preparations, such as Augustine had described, complete with despair, self-loathing, and turbulent emotions, followed by emotional conversions. In some Christian communities, this model has become virtually unvarying—to our own time. It is noteworthy that Augustine himself did not advocate this model of conversion. Indeed, as discussed in this chapter, he painstakingly detailed the several conversions that *together* altered his "way of feeling." Chapter 5, on Augustine's meditation, explores the practice by which Christian faith was woven into his life.

Considering Body

My doctoral dissertation, *Augustine on the Body* (2009 [1979]), traced Augustine's mature understanding of body, the result of his realization that the classical model of body as hierarchically arranged parts—body on the bottom, rational soul on top—was incompatible with the doctrines of creation, the incarnation of Jesus Christ, and the resurrection of body. Augustine sought to rehabilitate body as a permanent and essential part of human being, but he did so without proposing a different model of person. However, the most effective way to unseat an inadequate concept is not to heap criticisms on it in order to demonstrate its falseness or inadequacy, but rather to propose a new and more adequate concept.

Throughout his career as priest and bishop, Augustine endeavored to revise Christian ideas of body inherited from classical philosophy with fervent sound bites, such as the following:

> Perfect health of body will be the ultimate condition of the whole person.
>
> (*ep.* 118. 3. 14)

> We make up this whole: the flesh itself, which dies when the soul departs, is our weak part, and is not to be dismissed as to be fled from, but is placed aside to be received again, and when it is received it will be abandoned no more.
>
> (*cont.* 8. 19)

> You consider your flesh as fetters, but who loves his fetters? You consider the flesh a prison, but who loves his prison? No matter how great a master of the flesh you may be,... I think that you will close your eye if any blow threatens it.
>
> (*util. ieiun.* 3)

> Take away death, the last enemy, and my own flesh shall be my dear friend throughout eternity.
>
> (*s.* 115. 15)

> Is not our absorbing love of life really the soul's love for its body, a love which will haunt it until that body is returned to it risen and glorious?
>
> (*gn. litt.* 12. 35. 68)

Yet Augustine also frequently stated that mind is vastly superior to body. He had inherited the classical understanding—by

Augustine's time a popular truism—derived from Plato's *Apology*, that soul's immortality renders it unquestionably superior to the biodegradable body. Nor did he attempt to resolve the dissonance between his affirmative, even loving, statements about body and his frequent claims of the superiority of soul. Thus, his influence did not result in a restructured Christian model of the human person. Disparaging body (at best), and punishing it in real time (at worst), continued in the mainstream of Christian theology and philosophy, even in Augustine's own works.[4] His inconsistency illustrates Arnold Davidson's canny observation: "Automisms of attitude have a durability. A slow temporality, which does not match the sometimes rapid change of conceptual mutation. Mental habits have a tendency to inertia. And these habits resist change that, in retrospect, seem conceptually required" (2001: 191).

Like Augustine, for many years I did not find a useable alternative to understanding the human person as hierarchically stacked components. I had to be content with protesting the ancient "centaur model" of human beings, featuring a human's (rational) head and a beast's (lustful) body.[5] In the early 1990s, I discovered Maxine Sheets-Johnstone's concept of "person," which does not assume stacked parts, but an "intelligent body." Sheets-Johnstone argues that when the human person is thought of as components, no matter how they are stacked, "person" is lost. It is not simply that soul/mind and body are inseparable, she writes, but that "they" don't exist. The intelligent body, a single entity, operates as a whole, collected and expressed as a fundamental feeling toward life. This, I think, is the understanding of "person" that Augustine needed. Sheets-Johnstone writes,

> [The "intelligent," body,] is the body that we know directly in the context or process of being alive. It is the body with which we came into the world prior to science or technology telling us what we are made of, how we are put together, how that togetherness works …. The body that emerges from the womb alive and kicking is the primordial one. From the moment of birth that body is the center and origin of our being in the world. It is, in fact, our first world and reality.
>
> (Sheets-Johnstone, 2009: 20)

The intelligent body is born with the "knowledge" of when and how to acquire the life skills it needs, from expressing feeling (hunger, fright, instability) to moving (turning over, crawling, walking), to acquiring "memory, understanding, and will."[6]

Considering Conversion

When I first read the *Confessions* as a young person, like Augustine I was not happy *enough*. I married when I was eighteen; by the time I was twenty-two I had two children and a painful duodenal ulcer that threatened to perforate. I had little energy, few interests, and slight education. But I read. I became fascinated by psychoanalysis, reading all of Freud that had been translated into English, understanding little of what I read. A friend recommended a Rogerian psychotherapist who mainly sat back and listened. Being listened to was a novel experience for me, and very effective. I began to take classes at a nearby community college, then went on to the nearest state college. About this time I read Augustine's *Confessions*, intrigued by the urgency of feeling Augustine described. I *needed* to understand Augustine better, so I began graduate study, learned four languages while commuting between Berkeley and the several community colleges at which I taught a class. I continue to read Augustine *for life*.

Two experiences alerted me to noticing in Augustine's *Confessions* the topics I consider in this chapter. First, a painful and life-threatening condition required me to seek fundamental change in my "way of feeling." This vivid memory of difficult work over almost a decade led me to anticipate that Augustine would describe his conversion as a labor-intensive and lengthy process. And that is what I observed. It is there, in Augustine's vivid Latin, but I had read *Confessions* as a course requirement, an academic exercise, and had not "heard" the full extent of Augustine's long and bitter struggle. When l brought my own experience—my "bowl of blood"—to reading, the text collapsed into my immediacy.

My experience of psychotherapy and education suggested that major reorientations of life rarely happen all at once, but in many small increments consisting of altered choices, large and small.

Fundamental and lasting change usually takes time, often a great deal of time. My "conversion" from a lifestyle supporting a painful ulcer to "more life, love, and work"[7] is ongoing, made possible by an initial period of psychotherapy, education, and sustained by an ongoing practice of reading "promiscuously"—for life.

Second, childhood agonies over whether my religious experience fit the prototype of conversion assumed by the fundamentalist Christians with whom I grew up prompted me to seek, and to observe in Augustine's autobiography, another pattern of conversion, namely, a lifelong journey of *becoming Christian*, that is, a life committed to becoming a loving person, follower of the God-who-is-love, grounded in humility, and learning within and from the choices of daily life.

A young girl lies in her bed restless and tearful, terrified to go to sleep lest she die in the night and go to hell. I was that small girl. I had recently seen my first movie *ever*, not in a theater but at church. "The Missing Christian" depicts a young girl who is unsure of her religious beliefs. One morning she awakens to find that while she hesitated, the "Rapture" has occurred. Her family and friends, church members, indeed, all the good people on earth have been taken to heaven. She is left alone with the wicked people; she realizes that her eternal destination is hell.

On summer nights, lying in bed in a cold sweat, I imagined the cruel punishments and excruciating pains of hell. I thought I was a good *enough* girl, but I also recalled a number of recent misbehaviors that escalated into damnable sins in my mind as I lay in the dark. I had been baptized, but I knew, *I knew* that I had not asked for baptism in Christian obedience, but rather for "selfish" reasons: I wanted my parents' love, which would be mine in abundance if/when I responded to their hints that it was *time* for me to declare my personal faith by seeking baptism. At eleven years of age, I had already reached—and passed—the "age of accountability." Moreover, I wanted not only my parents' love, but also the praise and affection of the congregation my father pastored. And there was another, even more insidious, reason.

In our church, I had observed many baptisms in the baptistery painted to depict the Jordan River. On these occasions, I had noted that the white sheet serving as a baptismal robe clung revealingly to women's bodies as they emerged, dripping, from the baptistery. This observation prodded me to seek baptism while I still had a straight up-and-down body. I was on the brink of adolescence; it was *time*.

I knew that I had requested baptism for all the wrong reasons. I knew that being a good *enough* girl was not sufficient for salvation. I recognized that I had not *really* experienced the precisely calibrated drama of conversion that was expected, beginning with the powerful emotional experience of *compunction* not only over particular sins but, more essentially, over my sinful *nature*. I had not experienced profoundly enough the tears and feelings of worthlessness and terrible guilt that preceded forgiveness, ecstatic happiness, and new life.

I was the helpless victim of an accepted prototype of what conversion feels like, looks like. Beside the high drama of this model, established in the religious consciousness of generations of Christians, there was no other scenario. So I lay awake, afraid of dying in the night and going to hell. It took many years, many hours of psychotherapy, and a great deal of education before I understood with confidence that there is no approved script for becoming Christian, that "grace is not so poor a thing that it cannot present itself in any number of ways" (Robinson, 2008: 240). Since those long ago days, Augustine's words, emerging from his "own experience," comfort and encourage me.

4

Bodies, Pleasures, and the Young Augustine

Worth Dying For?

A value worth dying for is also a value worth living for, a value in which a nation, a community, or an individual's *sense of self* is so deeply invested that betrayal of that value is experienced as an irretrievable loss of self. Traditionally, religion and patriotism have been the primary values considered worth dying for: a belief, a nation, or an idea (such as freedom, democracy, or justice). Wars have produced hundreds of thousands of patriotic martyrs, and religious persecution continues to produce martyrs in some areas of the contemporary world.

However, in twenty-first-century North America, both religion and patriotism have lost currency as values "to die for." Religion is alive and well in private spheres, but lack of public respect for religious claims has created a vacuum that prompts the search for an alternative. Similarly, patriotism—"my nation, right or wrong"—has lost its persuasive power.

Yet there is apparently a perennial human need to ground the "self" in something greater than itself, a need prompted by "a gnawing feeling of lack" (Loy, 51), a "permanent identity crisis" (Berger, 74). Augustine recognized this need. In the first paragraph of his autobiography he wrote: "You [God] have made us for yourself, and our hearts are restless until they rest in you" (*conf*. 1. 1; my translation). Augustine's *Confessions* is an extended, detailed illustration and elaboration of this sentence, the story of his restless search for a resting place. His driven sexuality was a prominent feature of his search. Augustine's readers would like to know more—more than he tells us—about his search and its resolution. This chapter explores what can be known, and what must remain unknown, by considering two scholarly suggestions of what can be gathered from Augustine's descriptions of his search.

In contemporary North America, the phrase "to die for" is often trivialized, used to indicate strong approval, and randomly applied to anything from a car, to a dessert, to shoes. More seriously, the French philosopher Michel Foucault and others have suggested that in the late twentieth century, sexual orientation became, for many people, a self-identification, an ideology. Near the end of the twentieth century, Foucault wrote,

> It is through sex ... that each individual has ... access to his own intelligibility ... Hence the importance we ascribe to it, the reverential fear with which we surround it, the care we take to know it. It has become more important than our soul, more important almost than our life. (*Sexuality*, 156)

The qualifying gesture for anyone who does not share the social privilege of heteronormativity is "coming out," known in other circles as confession. Confession is "one of the West's most highly valued techniques for producing truth ... it is in the confession that truth and sex are joined.... From Christian penance to the present day, sex was a privileged theme of confession" (*Sexuality*, 59–61). One who declines to come out is thought of as betraying her/his *self*. Confession, on the other hand, is often experienced as profoundly freeing. In the twenty-first century, gender orientations and sexualities proliferate as individuals seek satisfying and meaningful self-identity. This is the social context in which contemporary historians' interest in Augustine's youthful sexuality occurs.

"One of the benefits of studying history is that it enables recognition of the strangeness of contemporary society" (Phillips and Reay, 3). We must begin by acknowledging the historical oddness of contemporary interest in self-identity based on sexuality:

> Sexuality in Western culture today has a centrality, an importance rarely true of other societies at other times in our history ... Our

tendency to define ourselves by our sexuality ... simply does not apply to most of the Western past.

(6–7)

The concept of "sexual orientation," defined as desire for particular sexual objects and acts, *did not exist* in Augustine's world. Moreover, the overriding importance of sex as revealing intimate and identifying aspects of the self was not a feature of Augustine's social and intellectual world. Augustine referred to sexuality simply as one current in "the river of human custom" (*flumen moris humani; conf.* 1. 6). Yet he repetitiously documented its well-nigh supreme importance in his youth, so that lacking sex, he said, he feared that he would not recognize himself. This seriousness and intensity contrast with, if not contradict, the abstraction that casually relegated sex to the "river of human custom."

Augustine has frequently been called the first modern man, usually based on his anxiety, or his "homesickness" within the gratifications on offer in his culture and society. Yet his resemblance to our own culture's consensus on the fluidity and significance of sexuality may be even more striking. Certainly, contemporary Western society's interest in gender and sexuality as primary ingredients in self-identity is strongly reminiscent of the young Augustine's insistence that sex was a major factor in his self-understanding.

Two Contemporary Interpretations

Present interpreters, influenced by the assumptions of contemporary North American and Western European social worlds, look to Augustine's sexual practices to provide what Peter Brown called a "uniquely resonant because symbolically precise clue" to understanding him (*Augustine and Sexuality*, 10). Two twenty-first-century interpretations of Augustine's sexuality will illustrate: Robin Lane Fox's *Augustine: Conversions to Confessions* (2015) and Geoffrey Rees's *The Romance of Innocent Sexuality* (2011). Lane Fox's book raises the question of what can be known of Augustine's sexuality; Rees explores Augustine's doctrine of original sin, finding in it theological justification for gay marriage.

In his book on the young Augustine, Fox discusses *Confessions* III.1. In this passage, Augustine states that as a young man, he "muddied the clear spring of friendship (*amicitia*) with the dirt of physical desire (*concupiscentia*) and clouded over its brightness with the dark hell of lust (*libido*)." He wrote: "It was a sweet thing to me both to love and to be loved, and more sweet still when I was able to enjoy the body of my lover" (*amare et amari dulce mihi erat magis, si et amantis corpore fruerer*). No friendship, he said, was free of his lust. Lane Fox struggles with the passage, cautiously concluding that since Augustine did not specify lust for a male friend, "he had sex with a lover, *surely* a female" (77). His rhetorical "surely" elides a multitude of assumptions and projections. Yet Augustine the rhetorician used words with intent and precision. And he *never spoke of a woman as a friend.*[1] As a bishop, he wrote many respectful letters to women about church business and spiritual matters, but he never called a woman a friend.

Friendship, in Augustine's homo*social* culture, was a male category, a relationship of persons considered equals. Describing the "original friendship" of Adam and Eve in his commentary on Genesis (*De genesi ad litteram,* roughly contemporary with his *Confessions*), Augustine thought of the good of marriage as reproduction; otherwise, he wrote, "how much more suitable it is for two (male) friends (*amici*) to dwell equally than for a man and a woman" (9. 5. 9).

In Augustine's voluminous writings no passage praising the friendship of a man and a woman matches in affection and detail his acclamation of male friendship:

> To talk and laugh and do kindnesses to each other; to read pleasant books together; to make jokes together and then talk seriously together; sometimes to disagree, but without any ill feeling, just as one may disagree with oneself. And to find that these disagreements made our general agreement all the sweeter; to be sometimes teaching and sometimes learning; to long impatiently for the absent and to welcome them with joy when they returned to us. These and other similar expressions of feeling, which proceed from the hearts of those who love and are loved in return, and are revealed in the face, the voice, the eyes, and in a thousand charming ways, were like a kindling fire to melt our souls together and out of many to make us one.
>
> (*conf.* 4. 8)

Although Augustine did not consider women as friends, his descriptions of his mother's piety and their shared experience of mystical transport reveal his deep respect and love for her. She had a masculine faith (*uirili fide*) in women's clothing (*mulierbri habitu*), Augustine wrote. After his conversion to celibacy she served Augustine's small company of retreatants with maternal love (*materna caritate*) and Christian goodness (*christiana pietate*; *conf*. 9. 4). Her "helicopter" devotion had irritated him in his youth, but the adult Augustine portrayed her with gratitude. Augustine did not think of her as a typical woman.

In marked contrast to his "concise and constrained" description of his woman partner, he wrote of his relationship with a male friend: "This friendship was a delight [literally 'sweet'] above all the delights of my life" (*suaui mihi super omnes suauitatis illius uitae mea; conf*. 4. 4). Augustine's readers have sometimes suggested that his "verbose and performatively passionate" description (Burrus et al., 25) implies that the young Augustine had male as well as female lovers. It cannot be assumed, however, that language that may suggest sexual ardor *to us* had a similar connotation in Augustine's social world.

In fact, Augustine used the same language to describe his enjoyment of God's friendship. Writing about his altered feeling shortly after his conversion to celibacy, stretched to the limits of language, he could find no more vivid way to describe his newfound pleasure in God than the "sweetness" he had experienced in human friendship. "How glad I was," he wrote, "to give up the things I had been so afraid to lose!"

> For you [God] cast them out from me, you true and supreme sweetness (*summa suauitas*); you cast them out and you entered in to me to take their place, sweeter than all pleasure.
>
> (*conf*. 9. 1)

Historians must be wary of projecting onto historical figures twentieth-century sexual language and assumptions.[2] Was Augustine bi-sexual? He described his sexual experiences simply as "bodies and pleasures" (*conf*. 3. 1). So then, what do we (think we) know about Augustine's sexual practices? Certainly his mature sexual choice was celibacy, preceded by a long sexual relationship with a woman. Prior to that: "bodies and pleasures." Since he did not further specify, we must not indulge in what may seem obvious to "us" (as individuals), or "us" (as a society). Reluctant as scholars are to say that we *don't know*, we must let it go at that, lest we become guilty of what Plato called "the double ignorance," namely, we "don't know, and [we] don't know that we don't know" (*Apology* 29a). Assignment of sexual proclivities to the young Augustine can only be projections of twenty-first-century Western European and North American assumptions.

Geoffrey Rees had a different agenda in his 2011 book *The Romance of Innocent Sexuality*. Rather than seeking to understand Augustine's sexual orientation, he enlisted Augustine's authority for help with a pressing contemporary question, namely, the legitimacy of gay marriage. Surprisingly, he identified in Augustine's elaboration of the doctrine of original sin theological support for gay marriage. According to Rees, the romance of innocent sexuality goes like this: alienated by sin from God, the source and guarantor of the self, sex seems to "*us*" (as a society) to be the feature by which the alienated self can be constituted and unified. We think within narratives, Rees writes, and according to the romance of innocent sexuality, marriage trumps original sin, rendering sex within marriage "innocent." In marriage, sex is to be practiced for reproduction, not for pleasure. Augustine notes that pleasure may occur, but must not be the point. *Concupiscentia*, the central mark of original sin, is "the genuine unity of humanity," the basis of human community. It follows, then, that if the married are exempt from the *community* of sinful humanity, human community is breached (Rees, 137).

Ironically, although Rees does not mention it, Augustine can also be considered the origin of the Christian version of "the romance of innocent sexuality." His discussion of friendship as "the great and natural good of humanity" in *De Genesi ad litteram* suggested that friendship between a man and a woman *is* possible in marriage, where the specter of original sin is bypassed. Writing *De bono coniugali*, he described marriage as "a kind of friendship, affection, and companionship" (1. 1). "The first natural link in human society is between man and wife," he said; the second link of human community is children.

Augustine's idea that marriage is the first bond of human community was a "startling innovation" from the ancient concept that friendship between men is of a "higher plane" than friendship between a man and a woman. As if to modify his audacity, Augustine quickly confirmed his agreement with ancient authorities that the politics of "friendship" between a man and a woman must consist of "the one governing and the other obeying " (Walsh, 2, n. 3).

Rees's sleight of hand occurs in his next step: rather than advocating that gay marriage should enjoy the same "innocence" as heterosexual marriage, he argues that *all* sexual expressions participate equally in original sin.[3] There is no innocent sexuality, no place to stand outside original sin—not in marriage, not even in celibacy (recall the proud virgins who are inferior to humble wives in Augustine's *De bono coniugali*). Rees sees in Augustine's doctrine of original sin the foundation for an inclusive community of sinners who recognize that they have no grounds for judging the consensual sexual practices of others. Participation in the human community, it then follows, should entail respectful and hospitable relationships with other sinners like oneself. Rees seeks to construct what he calls "an inclusively queer Augustinianism" (271), arguing for the "exclusion of all exclusion" from the community of sinners (289).

Augustine, however, does seem to be an unlikely exemplar of inclusion, as his doctrine of predestination demonstrates. In the last chapters of the *De ciuitate dei* (21. 9), Augustine envisioned the *massa damnata*, by far the largest human crowd, howling helplessly outside the gates, forever excluded from "the eternal felicity of the city of God in its perpetual Sabbath." The democracy Rees seeks in Augustine's doctrine of original sin is significantly, if not fatally, undermined by his insistence on the injustice—according to any human standard—of irrevocable, nonnegotiable predestination. Inequality of persons seemed "natural" to Augustine, not only in the present but also in eternal felicity; the only difference from present inequality he foresaw is that those with inferior allotments will not envy those with greater reward (*ciu*. 19. 14–16; 22. 30).

In short, neither assumptions about fourth-century sexual behavior based on twenty-first-century interpretations of fourth-century language, nor Augustine's purportedly gay-friendly theology can help us understand Augustine *in his historical context*. In contemporary Western societies, a heterosexual man does not usually confess to loving another man's "sweetness" (unless that man is his son or his father), but present usage is not a reliable clue to fourth-century conventions. Nor does Augustine's inclusive theology of original sin argue persuasively for gay marriage, though other grounds can be found in Augustine's writings to support this agenda.

Augustine Scholarship

For approximately the first five hundred years of the history of Christianity, theologians were pastors or pastor/bishops; for the next thousand years or so, theologians were monks; only in the most recent five hundred years have theologians been university or seminary professors. Theology itself alters dramatically in the context of the different lives in which it is understood and practiced. In the late twentieth and early twenty-first centuries, a different kind of Augustine scholarship began to appear in academic theology, namely, scholarship that acknowledges that Augustine was wrong about some things, that notices his inconsistencies and even contradictions, his occasional overstatement, imprecision, and evasiveness. This scholarship avoids both hagiography, on the one hand, and journalism based on "proof texts," on the other.

John Rist's chapter, "Augustinus Redevivus," in *Augustine: Ancient Thought Baptized* (1994) exemplifies scholarly willingness to rethink Augustine's interpretations of ancient doctrines. James O'Donnell, in *Augustine, Sinner and Saint* (2005), discusses Augustine's *fear*. It was fear, O'Donnell says, that inspired Augustine to write his confessions and fear that underlies his most characteristic doctrines and controversies: "When Augustine makes his most cherished assertions about his god, we need to hear that at the same time he is giving tacit voice to his deepest anxieties .... A seeker who does not share Augustine's questions and anxieties is unlikely to come to the same conception of god [sic]."

Augustine frequently quoted, "There is no fear in love, but perfect love casts out fear" (I John 4:18). This quotation may have shielded him from recognizing his fear, which then surreptitiously reappears, O'Donnell suggests, in his doctrines. Indeed, his "most original and nearly single-handed creation," the doctrine of original sin protects Augustine from understanding God as a tyrant who judges without mercy or attention to individual struggles (296, n. 25). For if *all* humans are worthy of damnation as Augustine declared, then God's great mercy in rescuing an elect few can become our focus. Indeed, the I John passage elides a more complex relationship between fear and love. It may be that love can *only* be increased by acknowledging our fears in order to redeem, *to carry over* the energy invested in them.

A second kind of Augustine scholarship presently occurring in academic contexts tacitly accepts consensus descriptions of Augustine's life and work and proceeds quickly to clarify fine points of his doctrines and teachings. Scholarship is usually done by individuals who have finely developed intellectual skills, and thus tend to have interest in, and identify with, Augustine the thinker. Aryeh Kosman writes: "We need to consider whether although something has been correctly argued, something has been lost sight of" (159). Contemporary scholarship often seems to imply by abeyance that Augustine's celibacy was retroactive; his youthful passion and how it segued in altered forms into his later life—his feeling—have been "lost sight of."

For roughly the last two centuries intellectual interests have dominated Augustinian studies, but for more than a thousand years between Augustine's lifetime and the nineteenth century, those who studied and interpreted Augustine's thought were primarily interested in his passion, evident most clearly in his practice of meditation (discussed in Chapter 5). Recall the many medieval and Renaissance paintings of St. Augustine with a flaming heart: "we are inflamed and we go," Augustine said (*"inardescimus et imus*; *conf.* 13. 9). Many of his readers were fascinated and instructed *by his on-location search for a method of weaving into daily life the longing expressed in* the fourth-century prayer of Serapion of Thmuis, "We beg you, make us truly alive." This Egyptian liturgical prayer, though he did not quote it (and may not have known it), succinctly expressed his longing, articulated again and again through idioms of fire. It could have been his prayer across every stage of his life from childhood to death. This is the Augustine medieval monks sought to channel as they imitated his practice of meditation.

Feminist theologians and historians have also criticized Augustine's treatment of women, both actual as self-reported and literary. Sometimes these objections are based on the "silent thought" or unexamined assumption that Augustine ought to share twenty-first century progressive values. The wide range of feminist criticisms will not be explored here. I mention only one that is both trenchant and nuanced. Carol Harrison finds in Augustine's writings "tantalizing hints of a more positive theology of women ... against a background largely determined by negative scriptural and social understandings" (175). Conflict between Augustine's "tantalizing hints" and the literary and social world within which he lived and thought produced inconsistency. Harrison writes: "Much of what [Augustine] says seems to be determined by ulterior factors which, though they often contradict his own independent thinking, are unthinkingly reiterated and allowed to influence his work, with no attempt to reconcile, or even articulate, the resulting contradictions" (169).

Harrison's suggestion, based as it is on impeccable scholarship, together with appreciation of the strength and beauty of Augustine's thought, identifies a problem shared by many authors, namely, a disconnect between an author's thoughtful interpretations and the durability of inherited assumptions. Unless and until an idea like equality is thoroughly integrated into all aspects of life, truisms of ideas and values—what Arnold Davidson calls "automisms of attitude" (91)—continue to exercise power to undermine conscious choices. Augustine's intellectual culture did not support the idea that all persons should be thought of and treated as equal. Indeed, fifteen hundred years later, "equality" is still a strongly contested idea, both in the abstract and, most damagingly, in the practices of contemporary societies.

Augustine's theology of love may exemplify this besetting human condition. To accept as a foundational principle "God is Love," not in the abstract but in the immediacy of ordinary life, is to undertake to follow the only exemplar we have of a perfectly loving human being, the humble Jesus who consented to wearing "our coats of skin." It is to undertake a commitment, not to *be* loving—which is beyond our ability to promise or to achieve—but, more realistically, to *become* loving, to "walk along the road" (*conf.* 7. 21). Becoming loving takes a lifetime. It took Augustine a lifetime. Stumbling reveals the human fallibility of one who is "walking along the road," but readily acknowledges that he has not "arrived" at his goal. Nevertheless, he has confidence that he is on the right road. Chapter 5 explores Augustine's practice of meditation as his long-term strategy for "walking along the road"; Chapter 6 considers Augustine's end-of-life reflections on his journey.

Recent reconsiderations of Augustine's authorship, together with historians' research on the social world of Roman late antiquity (especially North Africa) provide a more realistic picture of the world in which Augustine lived and thought than had formerly been available to his readers. In short, current research presents Augustine as a complex human being, like every human being simultaneously constrained and empowered—blindered *and* sensitized—by his intimate experience with family and friends, and his public world of church and empire.

Interpreting Augustine as incapable of error contradicts his own self-presentation, not only in the early books of his *Confessions* but also in his sermons, treatises, letters, and his *Retractationes*. Vilifying him as the author of a depressed and depressing worldview also fails to reveal a human being working conscientiously to make sense—as he repeatedly reminded his readers—of "my own experience." Both extremes are inadequate. Beyond hagiographical and denigrating interpretations, Augustine's readers can begin to see a human being *becoming loving*, even acknowledging "the bad and the good that I did," yet on his deathbed still feeling the need of repentance, presumably not only for his long-outlived youthful flailing, but for his life as a whole.

It seems, then, not only that Augustine can be a superb guide to the intimate dynamics of living a Christian life, but that he also provides a cautionary tale. His rhetorical skills—on occasion—served not only his preaching and his meditation, but also self-justification. O'Donnell observes, he was "loath to admit that he was ever distinctly *wrong* on a point of substance" (318). As Augustine learned, rhetorical skill is neutral; it could be used either to deceive others or to strengthen his chosen agenda. It could also be used to deceive the easiest person to deceive—oneself.

Moreover, although his *animus* in controversy can be at least partly attributed to the style and tone of theological controversy in his time and location, he also seemed to forget, from time to time, his own insistence that "the way is firstly humility, secondly humility, and thirdly humility" (*ep.* 118). In his *Retractationes*, written near the end of his life, he called the monk Jovinian a "monster" (2. 22) for suggesting that married life is equal to celibacy as a condition in which to exercise and develop a Christian life—not an accusation a humble man would make. He also referred to "the noisy, mindless puffing" of his fellow African, Tertullian (*De bono uiduitatis* 4. 6). He was not gentle in debate with fellow Christian theologians.

In the following section, I endeavor to reposition Augustine's sexuality, not in contemporary language and values, but in the language in which he "carried over" his passion, "scattered and spent" on sex and worldly success in his youth, into his adult life.

The Lust Problem and the Love Project

By his own account, the young Augustine had a lust problem. Unforgettably, he likened the subjective feeling of his disorderly early life to "the scratching of poisoned nails, [causing] feverish swellings, abscesses, and running sores" (*conf.* 3. 2). What he remembered, writing his confessions, was unrelieved suffering: "I was fettered happily in bonds of misery so that I might be beaten with rods of red-hot iron—the rods of jealousy and suspicions, and fears and angers and quarrels" (*conf.* 3. 1). He dramatically exaggerated the pain of the lust problem, even in its temporary satisfaction, in order to advocate by contrast its resolution.

Augustine's far-from-simple solution to the problem of lust was the love project. He advocated gathering the tremendous *energy,* the *urgency* of lust, and using *that very power*—with God's help—to transmogrify lust *into* love. Rather than endeavoring to suppress or kill lust, its strength was to be harvested and "carried over" (*feror*), redistributed to the love project. Augustine reported that sex, so consuming in his youth, became simply unimportant when he was able to embrace the stronger pleasure that reconfigured his attention and energy.

"My weight is my love; by it I am carried wherever I am carried," he wrote (*conf.* 13. 9). *Could* Augustine honestly say *pondeus meum amor meus* in his early forties when he wrote his confessions? In this passage, Augustine may have been describing a method and a goal rather than an achieved accomplishment. A sermon he preached several years after he completed the *Confessions* supports this suggestion. In (*The Usefulness of Fasting*) *De utilitate ieiunii,* dated 403–12 CE, Augustine quoted Paul, "By the grace of God,

I am what I am" (I Cor. 15. 10). Augustine's model and mentor, Augustine called Paul simply "the Apostle."

> When you hear these words [Augustine said], you seem to hear one who is, as it were, filled and perfected. But Paul goes on to say, "Not as though I had already attained or were already perfect. But one thing I do: forgetting the things that are behind, and stretching forth to those that are before, I press on ... to the goal of the supernal vocation of God in Jesus Christ."

He comments, "[Paul] is on the way; he is hungry; he wishes to be filled; he is anxious; he desires to arrive; he is *passionately inflamed*"(*util. ieiu.* 1). The mood is one of movement, urgency, and restless longing—he is on fire! But Augustine's suggestion that Paul was "passionately inflamed" is not supported by the scriptural passage which describes Paul as rather doggedly "pressing on." Augustine read the scriptural description of Paul's journey informed by his own experience, "we catch fire and we go" (*inardescimus et imus*). Augustine refers to this experience repeatedly in his *Confessions*. His own feeling, by which he sought to understand Paul, informed his sense that Paul was passionately "stretching" toward the *goal* of being able to say without qualification, "My weight is my love; by it I am carried wherever I am carried." In the meantime, Augustine wrote, "One is not only instructed so as to see you, but also so as to grow strong enough to lay hold (*teneat*) on you, and he who cannot see you for the distance, may yet walk along the road by which he will arrive and see you and lay hold on you" (*conf.* 7. 21).

As discussed in Chapter 3, there is textual tension between Augustine's account of his conversion to celibacy and his slow *process* of multiple conversions. Through this process he turned—God turned him, he said—from lust, from compulsive anxious grasping in the *fear* that something would be missed, to love. That process could also be described as getting over himself. First, "I relaxed a little from myself" (*cessaui de me paululum; conf.* 7. 14), permitting him to "breathe a little in you [God]" (*respire in te paululum; conf.* 13. 14), until at last he sighted the goal: "My weight is my love; by it I am carried wherever I am carried" (*pondus meum amor meus; eo feror quocumque feror; conf.* 13. 9).

Twenty-first-century media conceptions of love as something one passively "falls into" differ markedly from Augustine's insistence on love's activity. The Christian life Augustine described in sermons, letters, and treatises is one of daily patient attentiveness to discerning the loving response within the particularity of each circumstance in which one finds oneself. For Augustine, this *process* was going on long before, and continued long after, the famous moments in the garden. According to Augustine, love is not—or is not primarily— an emotion. It is, rather, active intentional participation in God's love: "Love has feet, which take us to the church, love has hands which give to the poor, love has eyes which give information regarding who is in need" (*ep. Io. tr.* 7. 10). Augustine described participation in God's love, not as a sudden climactic event, but as a daily *practice*. Augustine's meditation was the practice by which he nourished his journey.

Augustine's doctrine of love may be his *only* doctrine that was *not* developed in the heat of controversy. "God is love," he preached on I John 4:16: "If this were the one and only thing we heard from the voice of God's Spirit—'For God is love'—we should ask for nothing more" (*ep. Io. tr.* 7. 4). Moreover, it is not a question of how much God should be loved, and how much the neighbor: *all* love worthy of the name is participation in God-who-is-love.

> Does it then follow that he who loves his brother loves God also? Of necessity he must love God: of necessity he must love love itself. He cannot love his brother and not love love: he cannot help loving love. And if he loves love, he needs must love God: in loving love, he is loving God .... If God is love, whoever loves love, loves God ... for God is love.
>
> (*ep. Io. tr.* 8. 10)

When my son, Ric, was four, my father undertook to ascertain whether, as he suspected, I was not bringing my children up "right." He asked little Ric, "Do you love Jesus?" Ric, understanding that there was a right answer but not knowing what it was, looked around the room helplessly. His eye fell on me and, suddenly confident, he replied, "I love Mommy!" A perfect Augustinian answer, but alas, not the answer that pleased my father.

Love, it must be acknowledged, is arguably the most dangerous of Aug's doctrines because it can easily be appropriated to rationalize actions by a person who, as Cordelia remarked of King Lear, "hath ever known himself but slenderly." His famous "Love and do as you will" (*ep. Io. tr.* 7.8) has been notoriously misused by medieval tyrants, heretic persecutors, and witch burners in the Christian West. Augustine himself used this principle to urge that Donatist Christians should be coerced, *for their own good*, into communion with the North African Roman Church.

Reading Augustine: Augustine and Authority

Contemporary Augustine scholarship, I have suggested, usually presents Augustine more as an historical person responding to the bewildering welter of values, knowledges, and pressures of his time and place, than as an authority in Christian doctrines, practices, and morality. Has he then become for us simply a fellow human being, however intelligent and passionate? How is his centuries-long authority altered by a picture of an Augustine at once saturated by, and seeking to reconfigure, the assumptions and values he inherited? Let us step back for a moment to sketch a framework within which Augustine's usefulness for the present can be placed.

Daily media reports of public figures accused of racist or sexist remarks or actions are sensitizing us to enduring forms of social injustice to which many Westerners have long been oblivious. Public awareness of ideological indifference to human, animal, and ecological suffering is long overdue. The statements and actions of many of our political leaders are severely damaging our sense of *community*, the most precious and fragile commodity of human society. Media dissemination of information is undermined by the perennial evils of bias, greed, and blindness. A current widespread distrust of authority—much of it well-earned—is common. In this puzzling situation of inadequate and untrustworthy "information," the idea of authority must be reconstructed. Can Augustine help?

It must be acknowledged, I think, that Augustine did not always set a good example in the very qualities he praised most highly. As a recognized authority in the rather recently legitimate fourth-century Christian Church, he consistently escalated difference to threat and sought to eradicate it, either by argument or by government-supported legal action. Although the history of Christianity is usually described as a slow but inevitable process by which differences of belief and practice were excluded and exiled (at best), or executed (at worst), the history of the Christian movements is a history of doctrinal diversity. Unity, the hope and goal of Augustine's Church, was more or less achieved in Augustine's lifetime by exclusion and exile, with his support. Perhaps, in his social and ecclesiastical world, he *could not have done otherwise*.

But notice this: alongside Augustine's life as a preacher, a bishop, and a fighter of heresy, he wove a continuous rhetoric of love, a structure no less durable than an edifice, and still powerful in our own day. I do not use the word "rhetoric" pejoratively. As discussed in Chapter 5, Augustine found that he could use his rhetorical skills *both* to refine and strengthen his own discipline of meditation, and to communicate God's love to immediate hearers and distant readers he could not have imagined.

How can we think of this complex human being? Here, I must speak personally, neither urging nor apologizing for my perspective. It seems to me egregiously presumptuous to judge Augustine's engagements in a far-distant time and place that I have studied for many years and still acknowledge that I understand "but slenderly," namely, fourth- and fifth-century North Africa. Endeavoring to avoid the "double ignorance," I confess to the lesser evil, namely, ignorance: I know that I do not know. Furthermore, I doubt my ability, even in a lifetime twice as long as my own, to gather the detailed knowledge necessary to make an informed judgment on whether Augustine was "right" to support the imperial collaboration protecting the institutionalization of Roman Christianity.

However, I am too short of resources—too poor, Augustine would say—to consider my inability to judge Augustine's decisions and actions decisive as to whether his "love project" can be useful to me. Augustine's authority is a different kind of authority than that of a closely reasoned argument, or the slogan of a courageous activist, though both of these kinds of authority can be found in his thoughts and actions. His authority is the more humble and intimate authority of one who is "walking along the way," and willing to talk about what nourishes him and might also sustain his readers.

His commitment to the long *process* of becoming a loving person has altered—is altering—my life. There is no "authority" quite as powerfully convincing as that of a person who reveals his life to fellow pilgrims, known and unknown, in all its exposed fragility, acknowledged error, passion, and beauty. Finding Augustine's example powerful, I must humbly accept the ambiguity in accepting the companionship of a human being whose advice *en route* is a rich resource. In short, I am led by Augustine to understand the truth of my life as he understood the truth of his life: "You shall remember all the way by which the Lord thy God has led you through this wildness" (Deuteronomy 8.2).

Beginning with the question, what is worth dying/living for? I have considered several proposals, only to arrive where I began, with Augustine's answer, "You have made us for yourself, and our hearts are restless (*inquietum*) until they rest (*requiescat*) in you" (*conf.* 1. 1). Writing his *Confessions*, he demonstrated his starting point, now no longer abstract but concretized in the narrative detail, the *process* of his life toward "*pondeus meum amor meus.*"

In the following chapter, I consider Augustine's primary resource for "walking along the way" his practice of meditation.

5

Augustine's Meditation

The public St. Augustine, represented by his treatises, sermons, and letters, is the Augustine that has largely preoccupied scholars due, perhaps, to his formidable influence on doctrines and controversies. The private Augustine has been given short shrift. Yet it is the private Augustine, occupied throughout his life with transforming his psychic "weight" from fear to love, who offers suggestions and an example that can be helpful to others similarly engaged.

In order to retrieve the private Augustine, we must consider his practice of meditation, well-documented in his writings. Meditation was central to Augustine's practice of Christianity; he devoted intellectual and emotional resources to cultivating his life *before God*. Augustine proposed meditation as an exercise in humility, an antidote to "disputing by heated argument" scriptural passages that appear to be "incongruous and contradictory" (*ep.* 181).

First, some general observations on meditation in late antiquity and the Middle Ages; second, Augustine's description of his own practice.

Memory

Authors in late antiquity and the Middle Ages described meditation as organized, structured, and skilled, a practice of the self. Meditation was not done to relax, to lower blood pressure, or to achieve the health benefits advertised in our time. It may, indeed, have had these effects, but that was not why medieval monks meditated.

Meditation was not a rest cure; it was a religious practice, learned and developed over many years.

Twenty-first-century Europeans and North Americans are not unaware of the power of memories. Contemporary attention to memories occurs, however, not as a religious practice, but in a secular context, namely, as psychoanalysis and psychotherapy. In fact, there was a close historical relationship between psychoanalysis and religion. Sarah Winter has described "the institution of psychoanalytic knowledge." Sigmund Freud, founder of psychoanalysis, seeking a cultural and institutional niche for psychoanalysis, first attempted to establish it as an academic discipline. When that effort failed, he then endeavored, with greater success, to replace religion's claim to act as a "cure of souls," and substituting pastors with psychoanalysts (Winter, 1999: 173f).

In the clinical practice of psychoanalysis, recovery of memories freighted with emotions, and reliving of personal experience is central. Particular memories exist and are retained *because of* their association with strong emotions; if an incident or event does not produce emotions, it is not likely to be remembered. Unlike Augustine's collection of his memories into the story of his life, the contemporary purpose of recalling and re-experiencing memories is relief of psychic pain and the construction of a functional inner world.

Augustine's *Confessions* not only was a rigorous exercise in remembering and reliving, it also spelled out a new and more fruitful chronicle that gathered his experience and imbedded it in the narrative of God's leading in "both the bad and the good that I did." "In the huge court of my memory ... I encounter myself; I recall myself—what I have done, when and where I did it, and my feeling (*adfectus*) at the time" (*conf.* 10. 8). It is rare to have an opportunity to watch an individual in the process of organizing his memories, that is, himself (*et hoc ego ipse sum*); Augustine's *Confessions* offers such an opportunity.[1]

> By the act of thought we are ... collecting together things which memory did contain, though in a disorganized and scattered way, and by giving them our close attention we are arranging for them to be as it were stored up to hand in that same memory where previously they lay hidden, neglected, and dispersed, so that now

they will readily come forward to the mind that has become familiar with them.

(*conf*. 10. 11)

Augustine gathered not only the long series of his conversions, discussed in Chapter 3, into the cover story of his process of becoming Christian, but also his life from infancy forward. "I have become to myself a piece of difficult ground, not to be worked over without much sweat" (*conf*. 10. 16). Increasingly sensitive to the subtlety of God's action in his life, he understood that his process of becoming Christian began long before, and continued after, his conversion to celibacy. One remarkable example of a significant change long after his conversion to celibacy is his appraisal of the value of his youthful rhetorical training and practice.

Augustine on Rhetoric

When Augustine wrote *Confessions* in mid-life, he described his career as a teacher of rhetoric as part of his "slavery" to worldly success. "What had helped me in the past to bear my hard labor had been the desire to make money. That desire had now gone." Disdainfully, he called his classes a "talking shop" (*nundinis loquacitas*), where students received from his "professorship of lies" (*cathedra mendacii*), "material for arming their own madness." "I took money for instructing my pupils how to overcome other people by speechmaking." After his conversion to celibacy he was at pains—literally and metaphorically—to abandon his career. He described a mysterious and painful lung disease or weakness that required his immediate resignation (*conf*. 9. 2). In short, in *Confessions*, Augustine emphatically excluded his years of learning and teaching rhetoric from the cover story of God's intimate leading, considering his profession nothing but part of his obsession with worldly success.

Augustine acknowledged that he had learned many skills as a boy that were useful in his Christian ministry, such as speaking, reading, writing, and arithmetic. He appreciated his secular education, both general skills and reading authors like Cicero and Plotinus.

Gathering his training in rhetoric into his life story took longer than other conversions, occurring about two decades after his conversion to celibacy. Only then did he understand that, like his other secular skills, it could be "converted" into both his professional work as preacher and teacher, and his practice of meditation.

Several years before his death, St. Augustine undertook to review his published works. In his *Retractationes (Reconsiderations)*, Augustine critically reconsidered many of his publications, correcting infelicitous or, he feared, misleading language. He reread his writings in roughly chronological order, intending to include in his survey, not only treatises, but also his sermons and letters. However, distracted by other duties, having reviewed ninety-three of his publications, he abandoned the project in 427 CE, three years before his death. While he was working on the project, Augustine noticed that an earlier work, *De doctrina christiana (On Christian Doctrine)*, begun in 396 CE, remained unfinished; he interrupted his present project to finish it, completing book 3 and writing book 4 (*c.* 427 CE).

Clearly the older Augustine found his rhetorical training and the impact of Cicero on his life more influential than simply jump-starting him on his search for wisdom. He recognized that his life story was incomplete, omitting as it did a description of the relationship of his training in rhetoric to his preaching, teaching, authorship, and, most importantly, his relationship with his God. Remarkably, he arced back in memory over his middle years as bishop and author to gather even his pre-conversion experience, weaving it into his life narrative (*doct. chr.* 4. 3. 4).

Augustine realized that in turning away from Cicero and his own youthful career, he nevertheless brought his engagement with rhetoric with him. He acknowledged that eloquence can assist the goals of teaching and preaching; those who preach "dully, unevenly, and coldly" benefit hearers less, he said, than those who preach "acutely, ornately, and vehemently." In *cathecizandis rudibus (Teaching the Uninstructed)* he described his method of preaching as considering a scripture verse or passage "one piece at a time as though to loosen it up or expand it for inspection and wonder by the minds of the audience" (*cat. rud.* 3. 5).[2]

He was careful to note that eloquence must be subordinated to effective communication: "the speaker should not consider the eloquence of his teaching but only the clarity"; "there is no reason for speaking if what is said is not understood" (*doct. chr.* 4. 9). Indeed, throughout his ministry, rhetorical skills, though subordinated to scripture, informed his distinctive preaching style. He seldom—if ever—used his own words if a scriptural word or phrase would strengthen his thought, quoting scripture both to reinforce and to attest the truth of his thought. Yet Augustine also realized that scriptural proficiency alone is insufficient; preachers and teachers must also "look into the heart of scripture with the eye of their own hearts" (*doct. chr.* 4. 11).

As a Christian teacher and preacher, Augustine reversed his earlier evaluation of rhetoric; he now recognized the usefulness of rhetorical skills:

> Who would dare to say that truth should stand in the person of its defenders unarmed against lying, so that they who wish to urge falsehoods know how to make their listeners benevolent or attentive or docile in their presentation, while the defenders of truth are ignorant of that art? Should the [defenders of falsehood] speak briefly, clearly, and plausibly while the defenders of truth speak so that they tire their listeners, make themselves difficult to understand and what they have to say dubious? … Should [the defenders of falsehood] urging the minds of their listeners into error, ardently exhort them, moving them by speech so that they terrify, sadden, and exhilarate them, while the defenders of truth are sluggish, cold, and somnolent? Who is so foolish as to think that this is wisdom? While the faculty of eloquence, which is of great value in urging either evil or justice, is in itself indifferent, *why should it not be obtained for the uses of the good in the service of truth* if the evil usurp it for the winning of perverse and vain causes in defense of iniquity and error?
>
> (*doct. chr*. 4. 2; emphasis added)

He was finally able to recover this aspect of his experience—with a "different web of associations"—and different "emotional coloration," that is, within the story of God's overarching leading in his activities and circumstances (Carruthers, 1998: 53–4). Recognizing now the *neutrality* of rhetorical skill rather than focusing on its potential for deception, Augustine retrieved many years of his own experience. More importantly, he understood rhetoric to be useful not only professionally but at the very center of his life as a Christian, namely, in his practice of meditation. Augustine's rhetorical training deeply informed his ability to access the "eye" of his own heart.

Monastic Meditation

Mary Carruthers has written a vivid account of medieval monks' practice of meditation. Memory was essential to meditation; in fact, it is the feeling pervading a remembered moment or incident that makes it "memorable." The goal of monastic meditation was to salvage the emotional power of memory from its ability to undermine conscious choices, and to place it within a new narrative where it supports intentional choices.

Medieval meditation had two primary characteristics: intense concentration and strong emotions. Feeling (*adfectus*), the foundation of memory, prompted and supplied the energy for a meditative self-isolation that "supplants food, sleep, and daily routines, blocking external stimuli" (Carruthers, 1990: 200–1). In Western societies, it is common to understand rationality as separate—and to be carefully sequestered—from feeling. We must jettison this modern assumption if we are to begin to understand Augustine, his contemporaries, and his followers. Tears, understood as evidence of strong feeling, were considered essential to effective meditation. For medieval monks, the standard scenario for meditation was "lying prostrate and weeping 'in silence,' that is, in meditation" (Carruthers, 1998: 53). Carruthers comments: we cannot notice too strongly that "the impelling force, the energy for the journey, is emotional." She adds: "The kind of emotions needed for meditation were not tranquil," but "very strong emotions that both punctuated and wounded memory" (Carruthers, 1998: 103 n. 8).

Preaching on Psalm 6, St. Augustine emphasized that the function of tears in meditation is not merely to wash (*laudari*) but rather to cleanse or scour (*rigatio*) the soul (Andrée, 2017: 185). Augustine specified the kind of weeping needed for effective meditation, "a weeping that penetrates to the inside … [that reaches] all the way to the innermost part of the heart." For the monk, the role of tears in meditation is to obliterate memories of the "gratifications of the body and every worldly pleasure." The meditator, he said, must "free himself from that delight" in order to make way for greater pleasures (*ps.* 6. 7). Moreover, weeping is not a temporary exercise for the new meditator, but a permanent feature of meditation, for "the holier a man is, and the fuller of holy desire, so much the more abundant is his weeping when he prays" (*ciu.* 22. 17). The essential importance of tears in the medieval monastic practice of meditation is key to considering Augustine's deathbed tears, discussed in Chapter 6.

The first task of meditation was to create a theme or thesis that effectively identified and elicited memories, organizing discrete memories into parts of a whole. An adequate cover story moved memories into relationships, so that memories that had seemed to be isolated from one another are gathered in. The mental scheme that organized Augustine's self-understanding involved the actions of two agents, God's leading and Augustine's attentiveness, a difficult-to-articulate coordination that he was still straining to describe in his last writings. On the one hand, God's grace does it all; on the other, humans play a necessary role—a true cooperation, not something one agent does to another.[3]

For late antique and medieval meditators, "forgetting" was an essential part of organizing memories. Unlike "repression," in which painful memories are involuntarily expelled from consciousness, "forgetting" is intentional. It consists of placing a memory or cluster of memories in a different "location within a network … distributed through a different web of associations," and with different *emotional coloration* (Carruthers, 1998: 53–4). "Forgetting" is a kind of remembering, but remembering within a different and more productive setting.[4] For example, to "convert" his early rhetorical training Augustine lifted it from its earlier placement within his quest for "worldly success," repositioning it in a different "intention," with different "emotional coloration."

Far from erasing memories of sin, medieval monks recalled their sins in detail in order to stimulate penitence. "A monk who had completely forgotten himself by obliterating his own past would not be able to pray." After asking for forgiveness, the monk must "forget" his sins by moving them into a different location within the new configuration. In this way, St. Bernard wrote, sins "are no longer an obstacle to our salvation, but cooperate in our good" (quoted by Carruthers, 1998: 96). In meditation, even sins can be converted. Medieval monks learned this from Augustine. Placed within his narrative of God's leading, sins, however deplorable to the older Augustine, could be understood as necessary learning experiences.

A further feature of medieval meditation owes a great deal to the influence of rhetoric on Augustine—and to Augustine's influence on monastic meditation. *Ductus*, flow or motion, was a rhetorical concept indicating movement within and through the steps of a work's various parts. "*Ductus*, fueled by emotion, carries the meditator from one psychic place to another"; it is the journey by which "a composition guides a person to its various goals." These steps, we must notice, did not consist of a sequence of ideas or topics, but were rather "an affective, *emotional route from fear to joy*" populated by memories (Carruthers, 1998: 77–8, 80, n. 8; emphasis added). Throughout his Christian life, Augustine reconsidered and refined the steps through which he journeyed in meditation.

St. Augustine's Meditation

"I cannot even comprehend myself whom you have made; and yet in my meditation a fire flames out, so that I seek your face evermore" (*trin*. 15. 7. 13). Augustine had a long interest in developing an effective meditative program. About a year after his conversion to celibacy, an early treatise, *De quantitate animae* (*an. quant.*, 387–8 CE), lists seven steps, beginning with "the soul's care for its body" and culminating in "the vision and contemplation of truth."[5] Augustine mentioned fear at step four, simply to note that fear carries the danger of "lessening that tranquility which is essential in the investigation of obscure matters" (*an. quant.* xxxiii). After proposing stages or steps of the meditative journey, he suggested alternative steps in which memories of experiences of beauty are the *ductus* that moves the process. These steps, he said, are: "beauty from another thing; beauty through another thing; beauty about another thing; beauty towards the beautiful; beauty in the beautiful; beauty towards beauty; [and] beauty in beauty" (*an. quant.* xxv). In Augustine's earliest description of meditation, beauty was both the *ductus*—the map—and the goal of meditative practice.

However, a decade later when he began to write *On Christian Doctrine* (*doct. chr.*) Augustine had changed his mind about the role of fear in meditation. The carefully plotted steps he described in his subsequent writings *begin* with strongly evoked fear. Augustine, a fearful man,[6] had learned an essential *use* of fear, namely, *fear erases pride*: "Fear may inspire in us thought about our mortality and our inevitable future death, and, as our flesh begins to crawl (literally: breaks out in goose-flesh (horripilation; *clauatis carnibus*), nails all our pride to the wood of the cross" (*doct. chr.* II. 7. 9).[7] Augustine's embrace of humility, discussed in Chapter 1, favored any strategy that attacked pride, the enemy of humility; he had learned that fear effectively blocked pride.

The second step of meditation described in this early treatise is piety, by which we "believe that what is written [in scripture] is more beneficial and more accurate than … what we can know of ourselves."[8] The third step is knowledge, which is "nothing else except that God must be loved for his own sake and our neighbor for the sake of God … that is, that our entire love of our neighbor as also of ourselves is to be referred to God " (*doct. chr.*, II. 7. 10). The fourth step is strength, the fifth mercy; the sixth step is cleansing "the eye of the heart, whereby God may be seen." "It is through these steps," Augustine wrote, "that we make our way to [the seventh step], wisdom, peace, and serenity" (*doct. chr.* II. 7. 11).

In Augustine's mature writings, fear continued to be the first step in the meditative process. Indeed, evoking fear in its full strength *fuels* the meditative journey. Further steps both incorporate and transcend fear.[9] Augustine reiterated his meditative steps with slight variations in several writings. He quoted Psalm 111:10, "The fear of the Lord is the beginning of wisdom," adding, "If you don't want to be afraid, learn how to fear" (*s.* 348. 1). Again he described steps that begin with fear, ascend through piety to knowledge, courage, and mercy, to the cleansing of false values; together they lead to the seventh step, the "triumph of total security and peace in Christ." By "wending our way to God by these steps," he wrote, we climb to "a place of rest and peace."

A late treatise, *The Gift of Perseverance* (428–9 CE), reaffirms the usefulness of fear: "It is uncertain whether anyone has received the gift [of perseverance] as long as he is still alive."[10] Considering this, Augustine noted, "It is good to fear" (*perseu.* 19). Recognizing that fear may be deeply hidden, he said:

> Whoever does not want to fear, let him probe his inmost self. Do not just touch the surface; go down into yourself; reach into the farthest corner of your heart. Examine it with care: see there, whether a poisoned vein of the wasting love of the world still does not pulse, whether you are not moved by some physical desires, and are not caught in some law of the senses; whether you are never elated with empty boasting, never depressed by some vain anxiety; then only can you dare to announce that you are pure and crystal clear, when you have sifted everything in the deepest recesses of your inner being.[11]

Augustine's ninth homily on I John explores the psychodynamic of his longtime claim that fear is a necessary first step toward love. As was his habit when preaching, he sought an image that facilitates understanding. Often in Augustine's impromptu analogies, the image is homely; sometimes it even overwhelms the teaching it was meant to assist.

> Fear ... prepares the place for charity; but when charity has taken up its dwelling, the fear that had prepared the place for it is expelled. As one grows the other diminishes: as charity moves to the center, fear is driven outside.... But if there had been no fear, there is no way for charity to enter. When we sew a seam, the thread must be let in by the needle: the needle goes in first but it must come out if the thread is to follow. So fear takes hold upon the mind, but does not stay there, because the purpose of its entry was to let charity in.
>
> (Ninth Homily on I John 4)

Fear is the needle that punctures the psyche, providing a port of entry for love. Augustine liked this image; he repeated and strengthened it in one of his last sermons.

In brief, fear played a significant part in Augustine's writings and teachings. It had several important uses; it dissolved pride, concentrated the mind, and triggered memories of one's life. However, as discussed in Chapter 6, Augustine's thinking on the usefulness of fear changed at the end of his life.

Confessions as Meditation

Confessions can be understood as an extension of Augustine's practice of meditation, a detailed account of Augustine's life story, namely, that from infancy *God's omniscient and utterly trustworthy leading shaped both the apparently random circumstances and events of his life and his own actions.* This cover story inevitably affected his narrative, assigning more significance to some persons and events than to others, to his mother, for example, and not to his partner, the mother of his son. In *Confessions*, Augustine recalled his past and trusted God's leading in his future: "You will bear us up, yes, from our infancy until our grey hairs, you will bear us up" (*conf*. 4. 16).

Confessions is an extended meditation in which feeling-infused memories are recalled and reinterpreted as support for the cover story of his life. Just as medieval meditation recovered and gathered the particular detailed memories of the meditator, *Confessions* details Augustine's personal struggle to understand and to find the strength to live as a Christian (*doct. chr.* 3. 10. 15–16; also *ep.* 157. 2. 9).

Confessions employed two categories within which to collect the details of Augustine's life. His first category, the unrevised, unorganized, "unlaundered" account cannot be called a "story." It has no plot—no beginning, middle, and end. It is chaotic, now this, now that, a mixture of giddy pride and self-loathing, an aimless "whatever," a life that was "spilled and scattered," liquid, formless (*conf.* 11. 29), simultaneously restless and sluggish (*conf.* 8. 5). "My mind, which lay itching between my ears, was corrupted" (*conf.* 4. 8). In short, Augustine characterized his youth as lacking organization or goals—what Plato called "a miserable mass of unmixed messiness" (*Philebus* 1147e).

As he recalled his depressed and depressing youth, Augustine began to see the formation of a story. This story, the *story* of Augustine's life, emerging from chaos, was the content of his meditation. Why didn't he simply omit everything he could not gather into his narrative of becoming Christian? His images of restlessness, recklessness, and destitution effectively juxtapose the pandemonium and bankruptcy of his life to the redemptive miracle of God's leading. Augustine's bad behavior serves to highlight God's power. The incidents he recalled with repugnance appear in a different light when viewed as highlighting his theme.

God's activity in Augustine's life made sense of so much—his desires, his physical illnesses, his emotional and intellectual misery, even his "wandering desires" (*indagauerat uagus; conf.* 4. 2)—when he began to understand his life as the saga of God's activity: "You acted upon me" (*tu illud egisti, ... egisti ergo mecum; conf.* 5. 7–8). At times God was silent; sometimes God intervened dramatically, "breaking [his] bones with the rod of discipline" (*conf.* 6. 6). No room remains for Augustine's choices, no room for coincidence. For example, reconsidering his stated reason for moving to Rome from Carthage as a search for more considerate and appreciative students, he reinterpreted the move as God's prodding him to "change countries for the salvation of my soul." Again, as when he described his conversion to a spiritual universe (discussed in Chapter 3), Augustine offered two accounts, a personal account and a theological account. The theological account, God's leading, operated interior to Augustine's life: "In Carthage you prepared goads for me so that I should be driven from the place, and at Rome you provided attractions that would draw me there" (*conf.* 5. 8). Both accounts tell the same story; God worked within Augustine's feeling, *within* his choices (*ecce intus et ego foris; conf.* 10. 27). Again, one account is "accurate"; the other is the truth of his life; both are true.

Augustine's *Confessions* became a model of profound and honest self-revelation for medieval monastic meditation. To read his "autobiography" as meditative practice, readers must keep in mind the umbrella under which Augustine gathered "both the bad and the good that I did"—namely, that from infancy *God's omniscient and utterly trustworthy leading shaped the apparently random circumstances and events of his life.* This story excluded none of his experience, but it inevitably affected his narrative, assigning more significance to some persons and events than to others. Augustine trusted that God's management of his life would continue: "You will bear us up, yes, from our infancy until our grey hairs, you will bear us up" (*conf.* 4. 16). Augustine's *coniugium*, the focus of

Chapter 3, offers an especially striking example of St. Augustine's project of "laundering" his memories (*memoria munda*) and their repositioning in relation to his life story.

Reading Augustine

An author who seeks to "tell himself the story of his life" cannot avoid becoming aware that he is not the only character with a speaking part. At myriad points, the presence and influence of others are decisive. But *Confessions* is not a memoir written primarily to inform or edify readers; it is a meditation, an end in itself. Despite occasional nods to his readers—whether God, "the brothers," or others whose unsympathetic laughter he feared—it was not written primarily to be read. Rather, it is a revisiting, revisioning, and reorganizing of Augustine's life, a repurposing of its details into a new saga, retrieving from the scattershot of memory a perceptible pattern and trajectory.

Frustrations frequently expressed by Augustine's modern readers relate directly to Augustine's thesis. Twenty-first-century readers would like to know many things that, *within his governing agenda*, fade into the background or disappear altogether. I would like, for example, to have more information, and more of his reflection, on his *coniugium*. I wish Augustine had given even a brief nod to his partner's subjectivity by providing her name. But she, it seems, was relegated to the non-story of his random flailing and failing search for happiness. Indeed, Augustine himself introduced her in just this way, as "a woman who had come my way because of my wandering desires and my lack of considered judgment" (*conf.* 4. 2).

At a time when leaders of the Church were *not* writing memoirs exposing their youthful sins, Augustine acknowledged many temptations and misdeeds, integrating them into his story. But a careful reader will also take note that there remains a rather large humus pile of omissions—that is, experience that he could not fit into his life story. Augustine's fifteen-year intimate relationship with his partner, the mother of his son, is the most obvious of these omissions.

On the other hand, I need *not* know quite so much about his mother and her activities in his life. Yet her presence, in *Confessions* as in his life, indicates her significance in his story. In his youth she was, whether he recognized and appreciated it at the time or not, the *sine qua non* "voice of God" to him (*conf.* 2. 2). In fact, Augustine's account of God's interventions in his life was, not surprisingly, very similar to those of his mother; sometimes she gave him the silent treatment, sometimes she interfered aggressively with his decisions and actions, and sometimes she punished him. I would be content also with less about his long and painful struggle and vivid anguish, his violent metaphors of chains, slavery, and wounds dripping blood. But again, in Augustine's understanding, his extreme suffering belongs to his story; God's violence was precisely calibrated to his own stubborn recalcitrance. Approaching *Confessions* as an example of Augustine's extended meditation clarifies why some aspects of his experience are included, and others that seem significant to his present readers are either omitted or brushed to the blurred outer edges of his story.

In short, *Confessions* was not written primarily for its readers, especially not for readers fifteen hundred years later with vastly different sensibilities, social expectations, and intellectual assumptions and commitments. It was not written for critics of Augustine's doctrinal stances, nor for feminists who deplore his treatment of women. Augustine was a man of his time, his generation, and his social location. He was a bishop, endeavoring to fulfill his duties as pastor, monk, and judge in the ecclesiastical court, as well as participant in the theological controversies of his time. He said that he trembled at these responsibilities, duties that have not been discussed here; they were, however, a daily reality for Augustine. He did not have leisure for meditation; he prioritized it and *made time* for it.

Augustine was an amazingly revelatory author, allowing himself to be more vulnerable than we recognized when we thought of him as an authoritative bishop, sometime-irascible defender of doctrine, expositor of scripture, and enthusiastic celibate. Augustine exposed his inner life more fully than any author of his time. He revealed him*self* to readers' scrutiny, not only in his accounts of the cringe-worthy actions of his youth, but also in his most intimate thoughts and conversations with his God. "Show me myself," he prayed in meditation (*me ipsum mihi indica*; *conf.* 10. 37). In turn, he revealed the self revealed to him in meditation to his readers, inviting us to consider the whole Augustine, neither saint nor sinner, but irreducibly *both*.

Augustine credited his discovery of "God and the soul" largely to writing. "I must confess that I have learned many things that I never knew before just by writing" (*solil*.1. 1; *trin*. 3 *proem*). "I attempt to be one of those who write because they have made some progress, and who, by means of writing, make further progress" (*ep*. 143. 2). Writing is—or can be—a meditative practice. Like prayer, it is an exercise in articulating one*self*, sorting out one's thoughts and emotions, and identifying one's *feeling*. "Prayer, you know, you open up your thoughts, and then you can get a clear look at them. No point trying to hide anything" (Robinson, 2008: 132).

The commitment to "telling myself the story of my life" has been powerful and rewarding for me for many years. It has been said that writing is thinking; for me, writing is better than thinking. The more pressing thoughts are, the less they are organized; they interrupt each other, shouting for attention. Writing slows thinking for reflection. Like Augustine, I have learned many things by writing.

I notice a change in Augustine's topics and writing style in *Confessions*. In books 1 through 8, the writing is colorful and fast-paced, recalling and reproducing Augustine's desperation. His images are violent, physical, abrasive. In mid-book 9, and increasingly through books 10–13, the momentum of Augustine's prose slows, becoming thoughtful and calm. His topics are less personal; he is eager to orient himself within the greater human experience; he asks larger questions, seeking to understand the operations of time, memory, and creation. His tone is exploratory, inquisitive, curious. He has "relaxed a little from myself" (*cessavi de me paulum*; *conf*. 7. 14). Having discovered the *truth of himself*, he now has the leisure to *explore*. Rather than loudly demanding truth, he seeks to *know what he thinks*.

Writing is about discovering what one thinks and *feels*. As discussed in Chapter 1, "feeling," as Augustine used the word, is informed by intellect, emotions, body, and experience; it is focused by an object that attracts desire. When several objects are equally desirable, a person is hopelessly conflicted. The seventeenth-century English priest Thomas Traherne wrote: "We love we know not what, and therefore everything allures us" (*Centuries* 4. 16). Long before Augustine, Socrates put the dilemma differently. Assuming that each person is always in internal dialogue with himself, he stated his only requirement for thinking, self-agreement: "consistency with oneself ... its opposite, to be in contradiction with oneself, actually means becoming one's own adversary" (Arendt, 1971: 186). Augustine described the long road from being one's own adversary to self-consistency more vividly than anyone, in his time or ours.

Chapter 6 follows St. Augustine's practice of meditation in its last stage, his deathbed tears.

6

Augustine's Deathbed Tears

As Augustine was dying, Vandals laid siege to Hippo. Augustine saw the destruction of his life's work. One of his last letters contained advice to priests and bishops who consulted him concerning whether they were permitted to flee their ecclesiastical stations at the approach of the Vandals. A pastor to the end, St. Augustine's letter tirelessly considered the scriptures and precedents that seem to permit flight, concluding that clergy may flee only if "there are no longer any persons for whose sake they ought still to remain" (Possidius, *Uita* XXVIII, 113; XXX. 119). The siege of Hippo lasted fourteen months; Augustine died in the third month of the siege.

Possidius, Bishop of Calama, who lived in St. Augustine's household for almost forty years in "intimate and delightful friendship" (*familiariter ac dulcitur uixi*; Uita XXXI. 145), described Augustine's last days:

> In private conversations, Augustine told us that even praiseworthy Christians and bishops … should not leave this life without having done fitting and appropriate penance. And this he himself did in his last illness … For he commanded that the shortest penitential Psalms of David should be copied for him; as he lay in bed looking at these sheets hanging on the wall, he wept copiously and constantly (*ubertime et iugiter*) …. About ten days before he departed from the body he asked that no one should come in to him except when doctors came to examine him or when food was brought to him. This was observed and done, and he had all that time free for prayer.
>
> (*Uita* XXI, 140)

Why did Augustine request privacy in his last few days? Is this the same Augustine who in mid-life so insouciantly revealed his youthful sins to readers? Augustine the pastor, acutely sensitive to others' intellectual and spiritual needs, seems to have found it difficult or impossible to reflect on himself when distracted by others' questions and problems. He needed to be alone so that he could be "*by himself*,"[1] concentrated, undistracted by "the care of endangered souls."

Augustine was aware of his contemporary influence; he considered his own process of dying a teachable moment. Clearly, we do not know what Possidius did not know, namely, the particular content of Augustine's tears. We can, however, gather a suggestion from Augustine's own descriptions of how he was accustomed to commune with his God, namely, his meditative practice.

Possidius described Augustine's deathbed tears as penitential. Twenty-first-century readers, informed by a flattened definition of "penance" as simply sorrow for sins, are not likely immediately to grasp the richer connotation of "penitence" that Possidius may have assumed and taken for granted. Augustine's own descriptions of his practice of meditation suggest that his last tears were informed by a profound and complex range of feeling, composed of emotions from fear and repentance to gratitude, beauty, love, and praise.

The Old Augustine

The old Augustine has a bad press in the twenty-first century. Even loyal readers have found it difficult to appreciate his last embattled writings.[2] His doctrine of predestination, his identification of the transmission of original sin as occurring at the moment of conception, and his repetitive and pugnacious tone make for difficult reading. John Burnaby, who has been called "one of Augustine's most perceptive admirers" (Bonner 1962: 139), wrote, "Nearly all that Augustine wrote after his seventieth year is the work of a man whose energy has burnt itself out, whose love has grown cold" (Burnaby 2007: 231). Peter Brown's 1967 biography, *Augustine of Hippo*, characterized Augustine's late conflict with Julian as "an unintelligent slogging match." However, Brown amended his earlier judgment in the 2000 edition of the biography. Influenced by new evidence discovered by Johannes Divjak, Brown found rather that Augustine's last letters demonstrate "an inspired fussiness [and] heroic lack of measure when it came to the care of endangered souls" (Brown, 2000 [1967]: 466).

However, in addition to doctrinal controversy, the old St. Augustine was engaged in duties precisely appropriate to his time of life.[3] In the culture of the present academy, an endemic agism neglects to notice that (even) the lives of saints and scholars have a shape. A scholar's skills of later years consist less in groundbreaking new ideas than in collecting one's memories and in criticizing and clarifying one's ideas. The perspective of many years often affords insight unattainable in earlier years. The privileged vantage point of old age does not appear automatically, but is the result of eager and thoughtful learning throughout life; Augustine simply called this responsiveness to learning humility.

James O'Donnell has proposed the intriguing idea that St. Augustine's *Retractationes* (*Reconsiderations*) should be considered volume two of his autobiography. *Confessions,* volume one, describes the young Augustine as passionate seeker; *Retractationes*, volume two, establishes the mature Augustine as bishop, author, and defender of doctrine. But *Retractationes* exhibits none of the intellectual and emotional urgency of *Confessions*; Augustine did not weep as he reviewed his publications; he shed no tears over the mistakes, inadequate words and expressions, and the *ad hominem* arguments that pepper his writings. We must look beyond *Retractationes* for reflections in which he was engaged both intellectually and emotionally. I suggest that Augustine's deathbed tears might be considered a virtual volume three of his autobiography. "Volume three," regrettably but of necessity, not Augustine's direct account, nevertheless is important to our understanding of his life and work.

Augustine "by Himself"

Augustine marveled as he observed: "And men go abroad to wonder at the heights of mountains, the huge waves of the sea, the broad streams of rivers, the vastness of the ocean, the turnings of the stars—and they do not notice themselves." Augustine noticed himself; he identified "himself," not with what he thought, believed, or even what he did, but with his memory: "Great indeed is the power of memory! It is something terrifying, my God, a profound and infinite multiplicity, and this thing is I, myself" (*et hoc ego ipse sum*; *conf*. 10. 8). Augustine wrote, "memory itself is feeling" (*animus sit etiam ipsa memoria*; *conf*. 10. 14). *Animus* is the principle of life, specifically, the soul as the seat of feeling, the heart.[4] Memories are *memorable* because of the *feeling* they carry: "I am my memories."

Certainly, the "facts" of remembered experience are also recalled—selectively, and accurately or inaccurately. But the remembered scenarios are structures designed to house and shelter feeling. Augustine repeatedly asked himself, "What exactly was this feeling?" (*conf*. 2. 9). He referred to his youthful *self* as a heterogeneous mass of "spilled and scattered" memories: "and so it will be until all together I can flow into you, purified and molten by the power of your love ... and I shall stand and become set in you, formed in your truth" (*conf*. 11. 29–30).

His access to God's activity in his life was *through* memory: "I will go past this force of mine called memory; I will go beyond it so that I may draw nearer to you .... I mount up through my feeling (*per animum meum*) toward you who dwell above me ... for *I desire to reach you at the point from which you may be reached*" (*conf*. 10. 17; emphasis added). His feeling-saturated memory of God's agency in his life was the confident route by which Augustine approached God; through his memory, God's guidance could finally be *concretely* identified.

Only as a dying man did Augustine have *both* the memories of a lifetime in particular and specific detail, *and* the effective meditation by which the scattered fragments of his experience could coalesce into a *corpus*, a body, *himself*. And Augustine longed to see nothing less than himself, his life as formed and shepherded at every perilous juncture by God. Augustine had articulated his longing to know the truth of his life in one of his earliest writings, *Soliloquia* (*Soliloquies*), in which he stated adamantly that he was concerned solely with "God and the soul." The first eight books of *Confessions* sort through the raucous detail of his youth as evidence of God's leading. But his desire to know himself and God was only completed in his deathbed meditation.

The urgent task of self-knowledge and knowledge of God required Augustine's memories, his rhetorical discipline, and—not least—his *adfectus*, his *passio*. It is not surprising that Augustine decided to stop work on *Retractationes* in order to complete the last sections of *De doctrina christiana* (*On Christian doctrine*), sections in which he discussed the importance of rhetoric within his Christian life. As discussed in Chapter 5, it was not only in his preaching and teaching that his training in rhetoric was useful; rhetorical *method* also informed his meditation, the practice in which he encountered himself.

R. G. Collingwood's striking phrase, "the collapse into immediacy" calls attention to the fact that abstractions are of little use until, and unless, they are understood *in the life* of a reader or hearer. In writing his *Confessions*, Augustine gathered the events of his life into a compendium of the *truth* of his life, namely, God acting on him, God's agency *within* Augustine's choices. In his last days, Augustine saw, not two entities—his own intention and God's intervention—one agent acting on the other, but simply *his life,* the way it worked. In other words, the abstract theological account of Augustine's life *collapsed into* simply *the way it was*, no longer requiring trust, but now *seeing* God's leading *within both* the bad and the good; both were *necessary*.

Another way to say this is that on his deathbed Augustine saw that he had *never made a mistake*. Augustine would not express it this way, however, because—on the surface and in everyday speech—this would certainly be heard as prideful. Nevertheless, it could be recognized *intus* in astonished humility. Exquisitely aware of the vast difference between what could be acknowledged *intus* and how it was likely to be interpreted in common parlance, Augustine was wary of language that ignored that distinction. While the young Augustine thought he was making decisions and choices, *God was acting within those choices* patiently and unerringly guiding him (*intus eras et ego foris*; *conf.* 10. 27). Everything that he did that certainly *looked* like a mistake, even his sins, was a necessary part of his journey.[5]

Augustine's cover story, God's leading, was *more truthful* than the litany of incidents that he remembered. On his deathbed, Augustine was finally in possession of the experiences together with his *feeling* in the moments of his life. Theological truth "collapsed" into personal truth. Remarkably, his story also *covered* his whole life, the milk he drank as an infant, his studies, his youthful "bad," God's silence, his physical and mental pain, his restlessness, and the long slow rehabilitation of his feeling from fear to love, from restlessness to rest.

A late conversion to which readers have access through Augustine's own writings is a remarkable change in his evaluation of human bodies. In earlier writings, he did not call human bodies beautiful. He knew that bodies, as part of the natural world, were God's creation, but this knowledge remained abstract until, much later in his life, he *recognized* the beauty of human bodies. Until then, he did not understand the significance of human bodies, nor was he able to *see* bodies as beautiful.

It is noteworthy that even when recalling his youthful sexual desire he never claimed that he was seduced by beautiful bodies. He did not describe his "slavery" to sex as produced by the "objects" that attracted him; rather, he blamed his own self-generated desires. Augustine was unusual, perhaps *sui generis*, among patristic authors in not accusing actual women, their dress, hairstyles, and behavior of tempting him. Two female *figures*—not actual women—attracted him at different moments, the "bold woman in the allegory of Solomon" (*conf.* 3. 6) and Lady Continence (*conf.* 8. 11).

Bodies and Beauty

In an early treatise, *De quantitate animae* (388 CE), Augustine analyzed attentiveness to beauty as meditative steps. A decade later, in his *Confessions*, he asked created things to tell him about God, and "their answer was in their beauty" (*conf.* 10. 6). Still later, in a closely reasoned sermon on the gospel of John he said: "The way you are going is the same as the destination to which you are going" (*Io. eu. tr.13. 4*). Beauty, he suggested, can be both the *way* and the *goal* to the "beauty of all things beautiful" (*pulchritude pulchrorum*; *conf.* 3. 6). It was not until the writings of his last years, however, that he articulated the connection of the beauty of human bodies to the great beauty, "beauty so old and so new" (*conf.* 10. 6).

In mid-life he had understood intellectually that the beauty for which he longed was *only* to be found within. Yet the images with which he pictured transcendent beauty were mediated through the senses, mysteriously enhanced: light, music, fragrance, embraces, food. In *Confessions*, his only comment on the beauty of human bodies was a general appreciation for the beauty of creation, followed by a warning: "If bodies please you, praise God for them and turn your love back from them to their maker, lest you should displease him in being pleased by them" (*conf.* 4. 12). At that time, he was not yet able to see the beauty of the creator in human bodies, as he had seen the beauty of the creator in "blowing breezes, the heaven, the sun, moon, and stars" (*conf.* 10. 6). Augustine did not suggest that the beauty of human bodies must be included in gratitude for the beauty of creation.

Surprisingly, it was in attempting to imagine resurrection bodies that Augustine came to recognize the significance of present bodies. He began by insisting on the continuity of present bodies to resurrection bodies. Lacking experience or even second-hand reports of the phenomenon, Christ's risen body was his paradigm and proof of the permanence of human flesh and blood. Yet, until the last decade of his life, he refused to suggest exactly how this could be understood, responding evasively to queries on the subject: To question "as to where and in what manner the Lord's body is in heaven [he said] would be altogether overcurious (*curiosissimum*) and superfluous" (*supervaceneum*) (*f. et symb* 6). Even while affirming the continuity of present bodies with resurrected bodies, he emphasized their differences:

> If I were to say that the body would rise again to be hungry and thirsty, to be sick and to suffer, to be subject to corruption, you would be right in refusing to believe me .... The flesh will rise incorruptible; the flesh will rise without defect, without blemish, without mortality, without burden, and without weight.
>
> (*s.* 240. 3)

However, late in his life, Augustine came to a different understanding of the significance of bodies. Approximately three years before his death (427 CE), when he wrote the final chapters of *City of God*, he described present human bodies as characterized *essentially* by the "harmonious congruence between all their parts and the beauty in their mutual arrangement and correspondence" (*ciu.* 22. 24). Indeed, he continued, the great beauty of human bodies makes it impossible to discern "whether the major consideration in their creation was usefulness or beauty." He cited multiple examples of the beauty of bodies, almost burying his point in detail;

the "internal organs [he said] delight the mind with their rational beauty," possessing even "greater beauty than the visible beauty of the external body." Augustine noticed no "design flaws" in human bodies; in addition to the beauty of bodies, he also admired the "precision skills" in bodies' operation.

In the passage quoted above, Augustine's examples of beautiful bodies were taken from male bodies. He cited men's beards and nipples as bodily features that seemed to have no discernable use, and therefore must exist only for beauty. Yet it was the female body Augustine found most miraculous in its ability to give birth and nourish infants. Augustine suggested that a woman's power of birth-giving is "the closest thing we have to God's own miraculous act of creation" (Conybere, 2018: 192). He expressed astonishment at the miracle of birth, going so far, in a late homily, as to state that human birth is an even greater miracle than Christ's resurrection: "One man rises from the dead; all marvel; many are born daily, and no one marvels! If we thought about it a little more rationally, it is a more wonderful miracle for someone who did not exist just to be, than for someone who already existed to come back to life" (*Io. eu. tr.* 8. 1; *s.* 242). Augustine repeated this observation several times: "One dead man rose again, and people were struck dumb with amazement, while nobody marvels at those who did not exist being born every day" (*Io. eu. tr.* 9. 1). Coming from Augustine, considering human birth even more miraculous than Christ's resurrection seems shocking, yet far from reconsidering this suggestion, he repeated it in more than one homily.

Birth was a truly startling analogy to resurrection from the dead; why did it occur to Augustine? Augustine, who often said, as he considered scripture, that he understood many things through his own experience, may have thought of the birth of his son. Although he did not write directly about his *coniugium*, readers may notice possible references when, in the middle of a largely unscripted treatise or homily, he searched his mind for an apt metaphor.

In *De ciuitate dei* bodies, specifically female bodies, frame Augustine's massive epic of the human race. Book 1 begins with advice and encouragement to women who had been raped in the 410 CE Sack of Rome; book 22 closes with his insistence that female bodies will be retained in the glorified bodies of the resurrection.[6]

Defect (*uitium*) will be removed from [resurrected] bodies, and nature preserved. And the sex of a woman is not a defect, but nature. They will then be exempt from sexual intercourse and childbearing, but the female parts will nonetheless remain, accommodated, not to the old uses, but to a new beauty (*decorum nouo*).

(*ciu.* 22. 17)

Resurrection Bodies

When "not a few" Christians were saying that the promised perfection of body meant that women will achieve male bodies in the resurrection, Augustine insisted that female bodies are not part of the punishment of the human race but, like male bodies, are the good creation of God, and thus will be retained in the resurrection (*ciu.* 22. 17). In this passage, a preamble to Augustine's attempt to imagine resurrection bodies, he said that in the resurrection, bodies will no longer exist for backbreaking labor and painful childbearing, but *solely for beauty*. In the resurrection, present bodies, "real bodies"—he insisted—relieved of their "uses," will be "reduced"[7] to their essence, beauty:

> If now, in such great fragility of the flesh and in such weak operation of our members, such great beauty of body appears that it entices the passionate and stimulates the learned to investigate … how much more beautiful will the body be there where there will be no distracting lust (*illicit libidinosis*), no corruption, no unsightly deformity, no miserable necessity, but instead unending eternity, beautiful truth, and utmost happiness.
>
> (*s.* 243.8. 7)

The *permanent* beauty of bodies had become, for the old Augustine, urgent testimony to the beauty and generosity of the creator. Moreover, it is their beauty that *connects* present bodies and resurrection bodies. Body's present beauty is the foundation on which Augustine based his insistence on the consanguinity of resurrection bodies with present bodies.

Throughout his writings, Augustine's strongest association of beauty with a physical sense was vision. Insistent as he was that resurrection of bodies will occur "in this flesh that we wear and not some other," he struggled with the question of whether resurrected eyes will see God. Facing this quandary, he did not return to his youthful misconception that—because he had read that humans are made in God's image—God must have a corporeal body. Moreover, unable to use his "own experience" as an interpretive lens, he had only the resurrected Christ as depicted in scripture as a model. Indeed, he said, Jesus Christ, the mediator between God and humans, who shared our "coats of flesh," already *has* a resurrected body; it is humans who will change—beyond our wildest dreams—in the resurrection. He concluded that "our eyes will then have the power of seeing incorporeal things." He would like to go further: presently, the "eyes of the heart" see God, he suggested boldly, so perhaps it is not a stretch to presume that the "eyes of the body" will also see God on the day of resurrection.

Augustine was not satisfied with his rambling consideration of the question. Finally, he proposed an alternative: "and this is easier to accept—God will then be known to us and visible to us in such a way that we shall see him by the spirit in ourselves ... and also by the body we shall see him *in every body* to which the keen vision of the eye of the spiritual body shall extend" (*ciu.* 22. 29, emphasis added).

Reading Augustine

My reflections on reading Augustine usually appear at the end of each chapter. In this final chapter, however, Augustine must have the last word. I have acknowledged that my reading of Augustine owes a great deal to my experience; Augustine frequently acknowledged the same about his interpretation of scripture. I do not argue that my reading is more comprehensive, more accurate, or more profound than others' readings. What I can say is this: I have read Augustine *for life* for over fifty years, and this is what I see.

In his maturity and old age, St. Augustine *gathered* more and more of his experience into his understanding of God's leading. The old Augustine was awed by the created beauty of bodies, both male and female, and the miracle of human reproduction, which was first on his list of the blessings of human life (*ciu.* 22. 24). He did not, however, integrate his long relationship with his partner into the story of his life. He reported the existence of the relationship, but quite uncharacteristically did not reflect on it in any detail. To suggest reasons for this would be to resort to unsupported speculation and unwarranted projection. Yet the same Augustine said, "no surer step toward God can be imagined than love between human beings" (*mor.* 1. 26. 48). Thus I am puzzled that he did not consider his relationship with his partner as intimately affected by—and affecting—his understanding of God's loving agency in his life.

Why didn't Augustine consider his long relationship a veritable treasure for learning to love, and thus learning to love God? From his earliest to his later writings, he said that "everything capable of loving, loves God, whether knowingly or unknowingly" (*sol.* 1. 1, 386 CE). In a sermon on I John, preached almost three decades later (415 CE), Augustine said, "God is love"; he added, "and if this were the one and only thing we know about God, we should ask for nothing more" (*ep. Io. tr.* 7, 314). Anyone, he said, who loves, necessarily participates in God's love, for "God *is* love." I like to conjecture that if Augustine had lived a bit longer, he might have changed his mind about the relevance of his *coniugium* to God's loving direction of his life, as he was able to do with the value of rhetoric and the beauty of human bodies.

Home

Augustine's meditation consisted of steps within a theme that gathered from his memory evidence of God's leading throughout his life. His memory yielded something like a "God's eye view" of his life as a whole. No longer an abstraction, a carefully plotted story, or a matter of faith, on his deathbed, in his meditation, God's leading "collapsed into immediacy." The desperation of the young seeker resolved in his lifelong experience of God's guidance.

The penitential psalms at which the dying Augustine gazed, weeping—Psalms 6, 31, 129, and 142—dramatize the steps not only of his meditative practice, but also of his life experience. Each begins with the psalmist's consciousness of extreme vulnerability, physical and emotional suffering, and frightened awareness of dangerous enemies. The psalmist pleads for God's assistance. Each ends with confidence in, and gratitude for, God's love and mercy. "Why be afraid that he may desert you, that he may toss you aside in your old age, when your strength has failed? That is precisely the time when his strength will be in you, when your own is gone" (*ps.* 70. I. 11).

Augustine's long experience in meditation altered his understanding of the role of fear. In the earliest description of his practice of meditation, fear played no part. Yet in writings after 396 CE, he insisted on the importance of fear; fear was both the first step and the emotional energy—the strong *feeling*—that energized and guided meditation. The "first step" of any process is always ambiguous; on the one hand, it is essential, the *sine qua non* of the steps; yet it is also the lowest step.[8] In Augustine's homilies on I John, delivered to his congregation in Hippo during the Easter season 415 CE, Augustine thoughtfully analyzed the relationship of fear and love. Fear, he said, "prepares the place for love (*caritas*), but when love has taken up its dwelling, the fear that had created space for love is expelled. As one grows, the other diminishes; the greater the love, the lesser the fear. But if there has been no fear, there is no way for love to enter" (*Homilies on I. John, seventh homily* 4).

Shortly before his death, however, Augustine reported the disappearance of fear: "Fear should grow less the closer we approach to our home country," he said, and "those who are arriving [will have] no fear at all." "What has put fear out of the door [he said] is the love of God, whom you are loving with your whole heart and with your whole soul and with your whole mind" (s. 348. 3. 4). Fear of death, formerly invoked so strongly as to cause flesh to prickle, has vanished. In the "valley of the shadow of death," Augustine said, fear is overcome by love. One of Augustine's favorite and often-cited verses was I John 4:18: "There is no fear in love, but perfect love casts out fear." In short, fear has indispensable but temporary uses; fear is absorbed into love, and love puts fear "out the door."

> When my father lay dying, he struggled to say a single word. Finally my sister, bending close, thought she heard it: "Home,

Daddy? You want to go home?" He nodded. "But you *are* home," she said, "this is your home with Dennis and me." He shook his head, no. Then she understood: "You want to go home to Jesus, Daddy?" Now he nodded with all his remaining strength. "Home" was his last word.

At the time of his death, Augustine knew who he was before God, and he insisted on dying as that man, not as the seeker portrayed in *Confessions*, not as pastor or bishop, not as defender of doctrine. Soon after his conversion to celibacy he had identified the governing story of his life (*sol.* 1. 1). He began to construct this narrative in *Confessions*, but he completed it in meditation on his deathbed when he was at last in possession of the wealth of detailed memories that gave flesh to his narrative.

Augustine offered his practice of meditation as evidence that as love becomes capacious, meditation is no longer pushed, energized, and propelled by fear, but is attracted, drawn, *pulled* as by a magnet by love, a feeling no less strong, characterized by gratitude, peace, and beauty. Unlike fear, which is swallowed up into love, beauty is the enduring face of love: "Beauty grows in you with the growth of love; for love itself is the soul's beauty" (*Homilies* on I John 9:9). For Augustine, praise was the vocabulary—the activity—of profound gratitude.

From the first paragraph of *Confessions*, Augustine framed his narrative as an act of praise: "You arouse us to take pleasure in praising you, because you have made us for yourself, and our hearts are restless until they find rest in you" (*conf.* 1. 1). Augustine's deathbed tears were richly complex, penitential in the greater sense suggested by his practice of meditation. He was also profoundly moved by seeing his life as a whole, by recognizing God's patient and compassionate leading within "*both* the bad and the good that I did." And the beauty was overwhelming.

When our journey ends we return to our home.

(*ps.* 130. 14)

NOTES

Chapter 1

1 *Expositions of the Psalms* 1. 11; trans. Maria Boulding, 422.
2 Kosman, 202–3: "We misread Plato disastrously when we read him in light of a gnostic otherworldliness that pictures the forms as resident in a place far far away from ours, rather than as the principles of the intelligibility and being of this our sweet world....Throughout his writing, Plato is devoted to a philosophical vision designed to enable us to see things as they are."
3 Buber (1966: 74): "If a man has fulfilled the whole of the teaching and all the commandments but has not had the rapture and the inflaming, when he dies and passes beyond, paradise is opened to him, but because he has not felt rapture in the world, he does not feel it in paradise."
4 Carruthers (1998: 176) (n. 8); Carruthers recognized patterns in Augustine's postures and gestures reported in *conf.* 8. 12 that will later characterize medieval meditation, such as: "initial anguish expressed and maintained by continual weeping, mental imaging, repetition of Psalm *formulae*, and prone posture."
5 Predest. sanct. 6:"*Nostrum est enim credere et uelle, illius autem dare credendibus et uolentibus facultatem bene operandi per spiritum, per quem caritas diffunditur in cordibus nostris...quia ipse praeparat uolentatem, et utruque nostrum, quia non fit nisi uolentibus nobi...ut intellgatur quod et nos ea facimus, et Deus facit ut illa faciamus.*"

Chapter 2

1 In Augustine's society, his partner was called a "concubine," a term I translate in twenty-first-century usage as "partner." "Concubinage indicated ineligibility for marriage, usually due to class difference." Rawson (1974), 279.

2 *"Libido"* (lust) was usually used in classical Latin, *"concupiscentia"* in Christian Latin; Augustine used these terms interchangeably; *bon. coniug.*7, n. 19.
3 Celibacy should not be considered merely a sacrifice of sex, but a positive sexual decision, as Augustine's description of his decision makes very clear. For him, celibacy was a freedom. It is noteworthy that he did not urge his decision on anyone else, though he repeatedly recommended it as the "better way."
4 If either partner was likely to be unfaithful, it would have been Augustine, in the notorious sexual permissiveness for men in North African culture that he was "always" ranting about in his sermons. Men complained that Augustine constantly preached faithfulness in marriage; they called the subject his "hobby horse;" Ep. 259 1. 3; Meer (1961), 181.
5 Augustine's mother, Monica, is the only woman named in Augustine's writings. Lacking names, it is more difficult for readers to think of each woman as an individual with her own expectations, desires, and hopes. It cannot be claimed that this was Augustine's conscious strategy, but it is certainly a literary effect. It must also be noticed that failure to name someone with whom he was close does not necessarily reveal a lack of feeling; the friend whose death grieved Augustine so deeply is also unnamed (*conf.* 4. 4).
6 In the same year (373 CE) that Adeodatus was born, Augustine became a Manichaean; Manis allowed contraception and abortion on grounds that it is good to prevent the enfleshment of a soul. Later, Bishop Augustine argued against any method of contraception; *bono coniug.* 5. 5: "uel etiam opera aliquot malo agant ne nascantur." See also Noonan (1986), 125.
7 Augustine may have been referring to his former partner as he wrote (in *Ep.* 140. 19 (413), "In the case of a concubine, if she shall make profession that she will know no other man, although she be put away by him unto whom she is in subjection, she ought to be admitted to baptism." Walsh, "Introduction," *The Good of Marriage* (2001), xi ff.; Williams (1927).
8 Laeuchli (1972).
9 Julian of Eclanum accused Augustine's theory of original sin of promoting immorality: "because you blame defects of character on the filth of nature… no one needs to try to change," quoted by O'Donnell (2005), 282.

Chapter 3

1 *Conf.* 5. 10; 6. 4–5, 11. Reviewing his early writings Augustine found traces of this view and repeated his rejection of them (*Retract.* 2. 6).

2. Usually Augustine's *hominis erga hominem caritas* should be translated "person and person," but in this passage Augustine must intend "man and man" since he never called a woman a friend; see Chapter 4, n. 1.
3. In *Henderson the Rain King,* Saul Bellow describes a subjective voice that repeatedly demands, "I want, I want" but will not divulge *what* it wants. Similarly, Thomas Traherne, a sixteenth-century English priest, wrote: "We love we know not what, and so everything allures us," *Centuries* 4. 16.
4. Hannah Arendt, *Thinking* (1971): 163–4: Arendt comments on the "rather strange historical fact … that the ancient body-mind dichotomy with its strong hostility to the body could be adopted virtually intact by the Christian creed, which was based, after all, on the dogma of the incarnation and on belief in bodily resurrection, that is, on doctrines that should have spelled the end of the body-mind dichotomy and its unsolvable riddles."
5. Miles (2014).
6. Augustine's model for the Trinity was extrapolated from humans as image of God *in the mind*, a revision of his earlier misapprehension that if humans are image of God, God must be bodied, *trin.* XV. 7. 12.
7. Freud's criteria for psychic health (1952), 775.

Chapter 4

1. I am grateful to Catherine Conybeare for her observation that Augustine had no word with which to designate a woman friend that did not imply a sexual relationship; "*amicae*" referred to a mistress, "*amicitiae*" *also* implied a sexual relationship. He did not use the word "friendship" (*amicitia*) for his relationship with his mother (*conf.* 9. 4); see also Donald Burt, OSA (1991), "Friendship and Subordination in Earthly Societies," *AugStud* 22, 83–123.
2. We can, however, say what we think we see, so long as we are careful to designate where our suggestion lies on a continuum between speculation and secure documentation.
3. David G. Hunter (2003), "Augustine and the Making of Marriage in Roman North Africa," JECS 11, 1, 68: "What sin imported into human nature, what Adam and Eve lacked before their sin but experienced thereafter, was the unrestrained character of sexual desire … it is *lust*, not *sex, that is the problem*."

Chapter 5

1. Pierre Hadot (1995) wrote, "It is extremely rare to have the chance to see someone in the process of training himself to be a human being" *Philosophy*, 201.
2. Cameron, "Psychology of Augustine's Sermons," 66. Cameron describes Augustine's sermon style as "mastication of the text."
3. *Predest. sanct.* 6. 22: "For these things are both commanded us and are shown to be God's gifts in order that we may understand both that we do them, and that God makes us do them."
4. Carruthers (1998): 33–4; also 68–9 (n. 8).
5. Van Fleteren et al., *Mystic and Mystagogue,* especially Roland J. Teske, "St. Augustine and the Vision of God," 287–308 for discussion of the steps Augustine outlined in *an. quant.* XXXIII.70–6; also Antonio Tonna-Barthet OSA, "Augustinian Mystical Theology," 558–65.
6. *Conf.* repeatedly states St. Augustine's fear of being laughed at, from readers' laughter (I.9; 3.3; 4.1; 10.12) to God's laughter (6.6).
7. Carruthers (1998) notes that *clauatis*, an unusual adjective, refers to "the prickly surfaces of the shells of some mollusks," 302 n. 8.
8. Pascal *Pensées* I. VII. 65, 131. Pascal wrote: "The mystery furthest from our knowledge, that of the transmission of sin, [is] something without which we can have no knowledge of ourselves ….But for this mystery, the most incomprehensible of all, we remain incomprehensible to ourselves."
9. After Augustine had sent Darius a copy of *Confessions*, he entreated him, "When you find me in these pages, pray for me … pray, my son, pray. I feel deeply what I am saying; I know what I am asking … let all who have learned to love me, pray for me … pray for me" (*ep.* 231, c. 429 CE).
10. *Perseu.* 6. 12; Predestination is an "inscrutable" topic, Augustine says, one that must be left to God: "We live … more securely if we give the whole up to God, and do not entrust ourselves partly to him and partly to ourselves. God's ways, both in mercy and judgment, are past finding out" (9. 25).
11. Augustine described even the Last Judgment as a kind of self-judgment, based on memory: *ciu.* 20. 14.

Chapter 6

1. Hannah Arendt, *Thinking,* 187: "When Socrates goes home he is not alone; he is *by himself*." Arendt describes solitude as "that human

situation in which I keep myself company;" 185. "Alone," by contrast, connotes a lack of the company of others.
2. Greenblatt, "Invention," *New Yorker* (June 19, 2017). Contra: John C. Cavadini's argument that Augustine was the "true radical" against Julian's "sentimentalization of fallen human freedom"; "Marriage and Concupiscence," 189.
3. O'Donnell comments on the limits of contemporary biography: "Our biographical style ... knows the *bildungsroman* best, the narrative of youth and maturation. It does not know how to describe maturity and age, but struggles as best it can to impose its stereotypes." "Next Life," in Klingshim and Vessey, 222.
4. In Cassell's Latin Dictionary, the *first* definition of *animus* is "the spiritual or rational principle of life ... more specifically, the soul as the seat of feeling, the heart." Multiple quotations from Cicero illustrate this usage. A *secondary* definition is "the seat of thought, intellect, mind."
5. As St. Bernard wrote, sins can be "no longer an obstacle to our salvation, but contribute to our good," quoted by Carruthers (1998), 96.
6. Miles, "Rape to Resurrection," 75–92.
7. "*Reductio*" in medieval usage signified boiling a sauce to its essence without removing any of its ingredients, as in St. Bonaventure's *The Reduction of the Arts to Theology*.
8. Bonaventure sought to modify this ambiguity by stating that after climbing the steps of *The Mind's Road to God*, beginning with the natural world, the last and highest step is a recovery of all the steps together, creating the ultimate "stupor of wonder."

REFERENCES

Andrée, Alexander (2017), *"Tempus flendi et tempus ridendi,"* in *Tears, Sighs, and Laughter: Expressions of Emotions in the Middle Ages*. Per Fornegård, Erika Kihlman, Mia Åketsam, and Gunnel Engwall (eds). Stockholm: Kungl. Vitterhets historie och antikvitets akademien.

Arendt, Hannah (1971), *The Life of the Mind: One/Thinking: Two/Willing*. San Diego, CA: Harcourt.

Astell, Ann (2006), *Eating Beauty: The Eucharist and the Spiritual Arts of the Middle Ages*. Ithaca, NY: Cornell University Press.

Berger, Peter L. (1973), *The Homeless Mind: Modernization and Consciousness*. New York: Random.

Bonaventure, St. (1953 [1255]), *The Mind's Road to God*. Trans. George Boas. New York: Liberal Arts Library.

Bonner, Gerald (1962), "Libido and Concupiscentia in St. Augustine," *Studia Patristica*. 6, 303–14.

Brown, Peter (2000 [1967]), *Augustine of Hippo: A Biography*. Berkeley: University of California Press.

Buber, Martin (1966), *Hasidism and Modern Man*. New York: Harper and Row.

Burnaby, John (republished 2007), *Amor Dei: A Study of the Religion of Saint Augustine*. Eugene OR: Wipf and Stock.

Burrus, Virginia, Mark D. Jordan, and Karmen Mackendrick (2010), *Seducing Augustine: Bodies, Desires, and Confessions*. New York: Fordham University Press.

Cameron, Michael (2005), "*Totus Christus* and the Psychology of Augustine's Sermons," *AugStud*. 36 1, 66.

Carruthers, Mary (1990), *The Book of Memory*. New York: New York University Press.

Carruthers, Mary (1998), *The Craft of Thought: Meditation, Rhetoric, and the Making of Images, 400–1200*. New York: Cambridge University Press.

Cavadini, John C. (2017), "Reconsidering Augustine on Marriage and Concupiscence," *AugStud*. 48 1–2, 183–199.

Clausen, Ian (2018) *On Love, Confession, Surrender, and the Moral Self*. London: Bloomsbury.
Conybere, Catherine (2018), "The Creation of Eve," *AugStud*. 49 2, 181–98.
Davidson, Arnold (2001), *The Emergence of Sexuality: Historical Epistemology and the Formation of Concepts*. Cambridge, MA: Harvard University Press.
Dickens, Charles (1991 [1850]), *David Copperfield*. New York: Knopf.
Dreyfus, Hubert L., and Paul Rabinow (eds) (1983), *Michel Foucault: Beyond Structuralism and Hermeneutics*. Chicago, IL: University of Chicago Press.
Fleteren, Frederick, C. van Joseph, OSA Schnaubelt, and Joseph Reino (eds) (1994), *Augustine: Mysticand Mystigogue*. New York: Peter Lang.
Foucault, Michel (1980), *The History of Sexuality*. Trans. Robert Hurley. New York: Vintage.
Fox, Robin Lane (2015), *Augustine: Conversions to Confessions*. New York: Basic Books.
Freud, Sigmund (1952), *Civilization and Its Discontents*. Trans. Joan Rivere, in *The Major Works of Sigmund Freud*. Chicago, IL: Encyclopedia Britannica 54, 775.
Gadamer, Hans Georg (1975), *Truth and Method*. New York: Seabury, 310.
Gaines, James R. (1998), "Review of 'Rocket Boys: A Memoir,'" *The New York Times Book Review*. 10 1, 38.
Gilson, Etienne (1960), *The Christian Philosophy of St. Augustine*. New York: Random House.
Hadot, Pierre (1995), *Philosophy as a Way of Life*. Trans. Michael Chase. New York: Oxford.
Haraway, Donna (1997), "The Persistence of Vision," in *Writing on the Body: Embodiment and Feminist Theory*. Katie Conroy, Nadia Medina, and Sarah Atanbury (eds). New York: State University of New York Press, 289.
Harrison, Carol (2007), *Christian Truth and Fractured Humanity*. Oxford: Oxford University Press.
Hollingworth, Miles (2013), *St. Augustine of Hippo: An Intellectual Biography*. Oxford: Oxford University Press.
Hunter, David G. (2003), "Augustine and the Making of Marriage in Roman North Africa," *Journal of Early Christian Studies*. 11 1, 68.
Kosman, Aryeh (2013), *The Virtues of Thought*. Cambridge, MA: Harvard University Press.
Laeuchli, Samuel (1972), *Power and Sexuality in the Early Church*. Philadelphia, PA: Temple University Press.

Loy, David (1996). *Lack and Transcendence: The Problem of Death in Psychotherapy, Existentialism, and Buddhism.* New York: Humanity Books.

Meer, Frederic van der (1961), *Augustine the Bishop.* London: Sheed and Ward.

Miles, Margaret R. (1983), "Vision: The Eye of the Body and the Eye of the Mind in St. Augustine's *De trinitate* and the *Confessions,*" *Journal of Religion.* 63 2, 125–42.

Miles, Margaret R. (2007), "Not Nameless but Unnamed: The Woman Torn from Augustine's Side," in *Feminist Interpretations of Augustine*, Judith Stark (ed.). University Park: Pennsylvania State University Press, 167–88.

Miles, Margaret R. (2009 [1979]), *Augustine on the Body.* American Academy of Religion; republished, Eugene, OR: Cascade Books, Wipf and Stock.

Miles, Margaret R. (2012), "Augustine and Freud: The Secularization of Self-Deception," in *Augustine and Psychology.* Kim Paffenroth, Robert P. Kennedy, and John Doody (eds). Lantham, MD: Lexington Books, Rowman and Littlefield, 115–30.

Miles, Margaret R. (2012), "From Rape to Resurrection: Sin, Sexual Difference, and Politics," *Augustine's* City of God: *A Critical Guide.* New York: Cambridge University Press, 2012, 115–30.

Miles, Margaret R. (2014), *Beyond the Centaur: Imagining the Intelligent Body.* Eugene OR: Wipf and Stock.

Nagy, Piroska (2017), "The Power of Medieval Emotions," *Expressions of Emotions in the Middle Ages.* Per Fornegård, Erika Kihlman, Mia Åketsam, and Gunnel Engwall (eds). Stockholm: Kungl. Vitterhets historie och antikvitets akademien, 25.

Noonan, John (1986), *Contraception.* Cambridge, MA: Harvard University Press.

O'Donnell, James (2005), *Augustine, Sinner and Saint.* London: Profile Books.

Pascal, Blaise (1658 [1966]), *Pensées*, A. J. Krailsheimer, trans. Harmondsworth, UK: Penguin.

Phillips, Kim M., and Barry Reay (2002), *Sexualities in History.* New York: Routledge.

Plato (1961), *The Collected Dialogues of Plato.* Ed. Edith Hamilton and Huntington Cairns and trans. R. Hackforth. Princeton, NJ: Princeton University Press, Bollingen Series LXXI.

Plotinus, *The Enneads, vol. I*, A. H. Armstrong, trans. Loeb Classical Library. Cambridge, MA: Harvard University Press.

Rawson, Beryl (1974), "Roman Concubinage and Other *de facto* Marriages," in *Transactions of the American Philological Association.*

Douglas E. Gerber (ed.). Cleveland Ohio: Case Western Reserve University, 279.

Rees, Geoffrey (2011), *The Romance of Innocent Sexuality*. Eugene, OR: Cascade Books.

Richards, Mary Caroline (1970), *Centering in Pottery, Poetry, and the Person*. Middletown, CT: Weslyan University.

Rist, John (1994), *Augustine: Ancient Thought Baptized*. Cambridge: Cambridge University Press.

Robinson, Marilynne (2008), *Home*. New York: Farrar, Straus, and Giroux.

Rogoff, Irit (1992). "Tiny Anguishes: Reflections on Nagging, Scholastic Embarrassment, and Feminist Art History," *Differences* 4 3, 40.

Rousselle, Aline (1988), *Desire and the Body in Antiquity*. Oxford: Blackwell.

Sheets-Johnstone, Maxine (2009), *The Corporeal Turn: An Interdisciplinary Reader*. Exeter, UK: Imprint Academic.

Walsh, P. G. (ed. and trans.) (2001), *De bono coniugali; de sancta uirginitate*. Oxford: Clarendon Press.

Williams, N. P. (1927), *Ideas of the Fall and of Original Sin*. London: Longmans, Green.

Winter, Sarah (1999), *Freud and the Institution of Psychoanalytic Knowledge*. Stanford, CA: Stanford University Press.

INDEX

academics 35–6
Antony, St. 40, 45
asceticism 33–4
Augustine, St.
  autobiography, cover story 24, 75, 79, 83, 92–4
    "the bad and the good that I did" viii
    God's leading 24, 26, 37–8, 39, 83, 93, 101
  authority 22, 26, 68–71
  bishop 20, 22, 26–7
  "by himself" 91–2
  conversions 5–6, 33–9
    celibacy 5, 22, 41–3, 45, 67
    conversion as practice, process 68–71
    experience 3, 13–15, 20, 26, 28–30
    historical considerations 33–4
    humility 6–9
    interiority, 38, 93
    Jesus Christ 7, 38, 98
    scripture 36
    spiritual (incorporeal) universe 36–8
    validity of belief 35–6
  fire 1, 18, 25, 63, 67, A 80
  friends, friendship 24, 41–2, 45, 51–9, 61; God 58–9
  love theology 64, *see* love, fear to love
  mother 2, 6, 21, 24, 29, 59, 85–6
  partner 19–25, 27, 85, 99
  pain, illness 35, 46, 75, 86, 93
  penitence 90, 99–100
  son 23, 25, 45
  writing 87

becoming Christian 6, 33, 47–8, 51, 64, 67
bodies, human 43, 45–6, 48–51, 94–5
  beauty 94–6, 101
  feeling 5, 46–7
  female 27–8, 30, 53, 96–7
  intelligent body 50–1
  male 96
  resurrection 8, 49, 95, 97
  theology 48–51
  vision 96–8
beauty 9–17, 80–1, 93, 96–8
  classical philosophy 10
  feeling 5, 46–7
  link between creator and nature 11–12
  women 27–8, 30

Carruthers, Mary 77–80
celibacy 6, 21, 59
childbirth 25, 96, 99
Cicero 1, 33, 41, 75–6
Collingwood, R. G. 7, 93
Continence Lady 9, 44–5; girlfriends 44

INDEX

conversion, prototypes 48, 51–3, 82–3
creation. *See* beauty

death 89, 92–3, 99–100; praise 101
Descartes 14
desire 29, 38, 84
double ignorance 8, 60
"*ductus*", see rhetoric

experience 2, 13–16, 17, 22, 28–9

fear 62–3, 81–2, 100
feeling (singular) as self 1–4, 38, 43, 87, 92
  emotions 4–5, 74–8, 84
  feelings 2–3
fiction, drama 4–5

habit 6, 25, 30, 43–4
happiness/unhappiness 21, 34–5, 51–2
humility
  as learning posture 6–9, 30–1, 38–9, 81, 91
  and pride 7, 38–9

interpretation 13–15, 27–8, 65, 86, *see also* reading for life vi–x, 13–14, 17, 39–40, 46–7, 51–2, 98–9
Iovinian 34, 65

Julian of Eclanum, 29–30

Lane Fox, Robin 58
love 18, 21–2, 24–5
  fear to love 82, 94, 101
  lover 18, 22
lust (*concupiscentia*) 20, 22–3, 29, 43, 60, 66, *see also* original sin
  body 43–6

lust problem/love project 66–8
lust to love 60

marriage (*coniugali*) 6, 19–22, 23–7, 46
  Augustine's criteria 19
  gay marriage 60–1
meditation 73, 89, 100–1
  Augustine 80
  beauty 80–1
  Confessions 83–4, 91
  emotions 78
  fear 81–2, 100
  love 101
  monastic (medieval) 47–8, 63, 73, 78–80
  writing as meditative practice 87
memory/memories 73–4
  Augustine's 23, 27, 74, 92, 99
  feeling 92
  laundered, see rhetoric

Odyssey, Homer 13–14
old age 8, 90–1, 99–100
original sin 28–30, 61
  as feeling 29–30
  innocence 60–1

penitence 13, 79, 90, 101
Plato
  beauty 10
  double ignorance 7, 10, 50, 60, 83
  mixture 2
pleasure 4, 12, 22–3, 42, 57–9, 101
  sweetness 61
predestination 61–2
Possidius, Uita 89–90

pride 81. *See* Plato, double ignorance. *See also* humility
psychoanalysis/psychotherapy 16, 74. *See* happiness/unhappiness
  Freud 34–5, 74
punishment 34, 86. *See* pain

rationality 2, 5, 43
  and feeling 2–3, 78
reading (for life) vi–x, 13–14, 17, 39–40, 45, 47, 50, 98–9
  Augustine's ideal reader 17–18
  conversion by reading 40, *see also* feeling
Rees, Geoffrey 60–2
restlessness/rest x, 5, 44, 55–6
rhetoric 5, 35, 75–8, 93
  ductus 80
  forgetting, intentional 79
  meditation 95
  memory (laundered) 37, 83–5
  preaching 76–7

scholarship, Augustine 17, 61–4, 91
self 6, 42, 44, 52, 92
senses, (physical/spiritual) 11–12, 39, 47, 98
sex 6, 19–20, 25–7, 56–7
  sexual orientation 56
strength/weakness 7, 38

tears
  beauty 12–13
  deathbed 89–90
  male socialization 12, 44
  meditation 78–9

universalization (of experience) 28–30

will (*uoluntas*) 6
  divided 22, 29, 42–3
  and reason 42
  will power 9, 43–4
  worldly success 6, 21, 39–41, 45, 75